Beat the
SHARKS
At Their Own Game
When You Cash Out

**Follow the rules in this book and
put millions more in your pocket!**

By Steven G. Goldfarb

Editor: Roberta Moore
Book jacket design by Jennifer Wreisner
Interior design and layout by Brenda K. Bredahl, Word & Image

For more information, please write or fax to:
The North Harbor Press, Inc.
Post Office Box 11227
Chicago, IL 60611
facsimile (312) 946-0996
or contact your local bookstore.

Library of Congress Control No. 2001130108

ISBN 0-9707525-0-4

Acknowledgements

I would like to thank several people, whose help, support, and encouragement facilitated the writing of this book. I am grateful to my wife, Fran, who encouraged me to write this book. A special thanks to my good friend Rose Prock, whose assistance was vital; without her help, this book would never have been completed. I am indebted to my daughter-in-law Jennifer, who helped type the manuscript. I appreciate the help of my editor Roberta Moore, whose attention to detail and insistence on quality was invaluable in bringing this project to a conclusion. Finally, I want to thank my son Jay, who deserves special recognition for his contributions to the content and organization.

About the Author

Steven Goldfarb specializes in middle-market transactions in mergers and acquisitions, leveraged buyouts, and financings. Over the past 25 years, Mr. Goldfarb has worked on numerous transactions including initial public offerings of stock, stock-redemptions, public debt-offerings, private placements of debt, and the acquisition and sale of more than 75 companies. He is currently a managing director in the Investment Banking Department of a large regional securities firm. Mr. Goldfarb has a B.S. degree in accounting from Washington University in St. Louis and a J.D. degree from the St. Louis University School of Law.

Preface

Over the years, I have observed many transactions in which business owners left millions of dollars on the table when they sold their companies. Why did they leave this money on the table? Because they didn't possess the knowledge that would have enabled them to maximize the value of their businesses at the time of sale. This is why I decided to write this book. I want to share my knowledge and experience to provide you, the business owner, with some essential knowledge that will help you maximize value when you sell your company.

For simplicity, this knowledge has been organized into four parts. Parts I and II give you a set of rules that guide you through the pre-sale and sale process. Part III provides an explanation of the sale process, guidelines on how to select a mergers-and-acquisitions advisor (M&A advisor), and an in-depth analysis and evaluation of the kinds of structures of deals you may need to consider. Throughout the text, I have included scenarios of transactions in which I was involved as the advisor on mergers and acquisitions. These true-life examples (with names and certain facts changed to protect the confidentiality of my clients) will give you additional insights into the strategies I have set forth.

Why You Should Read This Book

How is my book different from the others you might find on this same topic? First, it was written specifically for the business owner and it contains critical information that has been proven to maximize the selling price of your business. Most other books on selling businesses are written by accountants or lawyers, and as you would expect, they typically focus on their authors' areas of expertise. While they contain detailed narratives exploring complicated accounting and legal issues, none of this information will help you to get one dollar more for your business.

Furthermore, these are the issues that lawyers and accountants are hired to deal with. As you will see clearly when you read this book, lawyers and accountants perform important functions that are critical to closing the sale, but these activities have nothing to do with determining the selling price of your business. In fact, the price is completely determined before these advisors get involved in the sale process.

This book focuses on what you, the business owner, can do to prepare and market your business to ensure that you get top dollar at the time of sale. One more important point: throughout this book, I emphasize the value of retaining a professional Mergers & Acquisitions advisor to assist you with the sale of your business. Why? Because it is highly improbable that you will be able to sell your business for as high a price as would be obtainable by an experienced Mergers & Acquisitions advisor. After reading this book, you will see why the difference in selling price will more than offset the fee. Furthermore, your advisor will handle the transaction while you continue to do what you do best — and what is best for getting the most value at the time of sale — which is running your business.

By following the rules in this book, and by hiring a competent Mergers & Acquisitions professional, you can put millions more in your pocket when you cash out. ⌒

TABLE OF CONTENTS

INTRODUCTION   1

PART I: What To Do Before Starting the Sale Process   3

Rule 1.   Prepare your company for sale. The highest
          prices are always paid to owners who engage
          in pre-sale planning.   5

Rule 2.   Make sure financial statements position your business
          in the most positive manner possible.   15

Rule 3.   Don't worry about income taxes. Do everything you
          can to maximize earnings.   25

Rule 4.   Don't milk the net worth out of your business prior
          to sale.   29

Rule 5.   Do not sell your business only when you are ready.
          Sell when market conditions are peaking and the
          future looks the brightest.   31

Rule 6.   Select the right mergers-and-acquisitions advisor
          to represent your company.   35

PART II: Rules To Follow During the Sale Process   41

Rule 7.   Do not try to sell the business yourself.   43

Rule 8.   Never state an asking price for the business.   47

Rule 9.   Sell through a competitive auctioning process
involving multiple buyers.   49

Rule 10.   Expand your search for buyers beyond your
competitors and known synergistic buyers.   51

Rule 11.   Sell the future, not the past.   53

Rule 12.   Educate yourself on the types of buyers in the
market and how to find them.   57

Rule 13.   Obtain the highest possible price for your business
by selling to a premium buyer.   65

Rule 14.   Understand the buyer's mentality.   71

Rule 15.   Do not sell to employees or competitors.   73

Rule 16.   Keep the sale process confidential.   77

PART III: What You Need To Know During the Sale
Process   83

Section 1:   Issues that could cause your sale to fail   85

Section 2:   How to sell without an asking price   91

Section 3:   The sale process   99

Section 4:   Key steps in the sale process   105

Section 5:   How deals are structured   111

Section 6:   The most common structures for deals and
             how I rate those structures   115

Section 7:   The final message   131

Table: Summary of the factors that maximize the
       value of a business   136

Glossary of terms used in mergers and acquisitions   139

Appendix A: Checklist for "due diligence"   144

Appendix B: Example of a Memorandum of
            Information   154

Introduction

Businesses are sold for many reasons. A sole shareholder, a family, or a small group of individuals who founded a business may have the bulk of their assets in the shares of a company. Sale of these shares for cash or in exchange for shares of a publicly traded company can satisfy needs of shareholders, such as paying off personal creditors, diversifying investments, providing for retirement, paying estate taxes, or providing for the owners' families who may or may not be active in the business. In other situations entrepreneurs who are good at starting companies find that they do not want to deal with or are unable to cope with the burdens of management that come with an emerging or maturing company. A sale can provide the necessary exit-vehicle and some immediate cash to allow the entrepreneur to start another company or retire.

In some cases, businesses are sold in order to solve serious internal or external problems. For example, if the shareholders of a closely held corporation cannot agree on certain major issues, and one faction is unable or unwilling to buy out the other, a sale to a third party may be the only solution. In other cases, changes in the marketplace, increased competition, rapidly changing technology, or obsolescence of the product may create a need for capital that the owners cannot supply or obtain. A sale to a larger concern may be the answer. Finally, many businesses are sold merely because the buyer makes the seller an offer that is too good to refuse, or because the seller recognizes the existence of a significant opportunity for a larger "score" by joining with a larger, more successful organization, or both.

Regardless of the principal motivations a business owner may have for selling, most owners have typically spent years of their adult life building their businesses. In building a business, an owner creates substantial net worth, but in most cases that net worth is not liquid but is tied up in the value of the business. For most entrepreneurs, almost all of their estate is contained in the value of their company. Nevertheless, it is a fact that most entrepreneurs pay more attention to maximizing value in the sale of their home than they do to maximizing value in the sale of their business.

Consider what you would do if you planned to sell your home and there was no dire urgency in regard to timing. First, you would do all of the preparations — including fix-up work that may be necessary to prepare the house for the market so that it would show at its best and attract the best offers. Then, you would put the home on the market at the time of the year that is known to be best for maximizing value. Finally, you would not undertake to sell the home yourself. Instead you would retain a professional real estate broker with the expertise to bring in multiple buyers and provide you with the highest price.

Now, let's look at how the majority of entrepreneurs view the sale of a business, that may contain almost all of their net worth. First, most entrepreneurs sell their businesses when *they* are ready, not when the business or the market is ready. Their decision to sell rarely reflects opportunities created by strong market conditions when the condition of the business is at its peak. The result is that, unless the owner's timing is coincidental with peak market conditions, the business will not be sold at the time when its value could be maximized. Market conditions and the impact of the market on the transaction are totally ignored.

Next, entrepreneurs rarely prepare their businesses for sale in the same way they would fix up their homes. Seldom do they engage in pre-sale planning to position the business in a way that would increase its attractiveness and maximize its value. Finally, many entrepreneurs make the mistake of believing that they can sell their businesses themselves. In the case of their homes, they would rely on a professional real estate broker, but in the case of their business, they feel that they understand it better and know who the buyer should be. This logic leads them to direct the execution of a transaction far more complicated than a real estate transaction. Even if they are successful in selling their businesses themselves, the usual result is that they end up with less than the maximum value in selling price. And, typically, the transaction contains less cash than they could have obtained and a substantial amount of deal structure that is less desirable.

The information in this book will help you avoid these pitfalls. First, it gives you a step-by-step process for maximizing the value of your business. Then it outlines the criteria you should look for in finding a Mergers & Acquisitions consultant to ensure that the value is realized. And finally, it provides critical tools and examples that you can use to guide you through the sale process, no matter what type of business you own. ⌁

PART I

What to do
BEFORE
Starting the
Sale Process

RULE 1

Prepare your company for sale. The highest prices are always paid to owners who engage in pre-sale planning.

Did you buy this book because you're ready to sell your business now and you want to proceed to get the best possible price? If so, stop for a minute and ask yourself a question: Is my business in the best possible condition for me to get the best possible price? As an expert, I can almost guarantee you that it is not. There are many things you can do that will increase the value of your company.

After you finish reading this book, please take my advice and retain a professional mergers-and-acquisitions advisor to help you prepare your company for sale. As a prerequisite, Rule 1 will walk you through the most important steps for preparation. These initial steps are very much like the process you would follow if you had decided to sell your home. The first thing you would do is assess what improvements would make it most attractive to a buyer at the highest possible price. You would do all of the appropriate cleaning up and fixing up — including hiring some outside expertise. In short, you would do whatever is needed to create a "perfect" home to show to prospective purchasers — *before putting it on the market.* Such attention is critical. It creates value and increases the buyer's level of desire for your house.

Why should it be any different with your business? Simply ask yourself: "What do I have to do to make my business as attractive as possible when I put it on the market?" There is one big difference, though, in the two situations. Getting a home ready for sale can be done within *two to three months* before marketing. In the case of a business, the planning or "getting ready" process should begin *two to three years* before marketing the business. This is because the most significant things you can do to make your business as attractive as possible to potential buyers are things that must be done over a period of time. You may already have some of them in place or close at hand. Others will require some adjustments in your business practices. The duration of the "getting ready" process can be compressed significantly to accommodate whatever timetable you need to follow from now until your business is sold, but keep in mind that the more time you allow, the greater the value you can create.

Make Sure Your Historical Financial Statements Maximize Reported Profits

Potential buyers of your business will determine your company's future profitability by examining current and historical financial statements — this is the best reference they can use. Put simply, *your historical financial statements will determine your company's value.* These are the primary tools used by buyers to place value on a business. Once you have completed these statements, you have to live with them. They cannot be changed retroactively. There are some key business practices that dictate what your company's financial statements look like. It is likely that you will need to make some necessary adjustments to these practices in order to create a direct correlation between maximizing profitability on your historical financial statements and maximizing the value of your business at the time of sale. These adjustments include the following three recommended practices.

1. Stop using aggressive accounting practices.
My more than 20 years in the mergers-and-acquisitions business have taught me a great deal, and one thing I've learned is this: Entrepreneurs HATE to pay taxes. So they make aggressive, concerted efforts to reduce the earnings reported on their books as much as possible in order to reduce their income tax burden. Typical examples of aggressive accounting used to reduce taxes are:
   ◆ "expensing" items that should be capitalized and depreciated,
   ◆ writing off existing inventory that is still good and usable,

◆ taking out as expenses various "perks," high salaries and bonuses and, to the extent possible, having personal expenses paid by the company.

Such aggressive accounting practices always reduce the liability of a business owner for income taxes, but continuing such practices until the time of sale can result in a reduction in the value of the business. It also may create other problems that will impact the ability to sell the company.

HOW VALUE CAN BE REDUCED THROUGH AGGRESSIVE TAX-ACCOUNTING PROCEDURES			
	Year of Sale		
	1989	1990	1991
Actual business income (000)	$1,200	$1,400	$1,600
Reductions in income due to aggressive tax accounting practices			
Expensing of capitalized items	$125	$150	$200
Write-down of good inventory	$400	$450	$500
Personal expenses paid by the company	$50	$75	$90
Taxable income	$625	$725	$810

Assuming this is a Sub-Chapter S corporation, the owner's accounting practices would reduce operating profit by $790,000 and save $316,000 in personal income taxes in the year of sale. However, if the buyer is valuing this business at six times the operating profit, a $790,000 reduction in profit on the books could reduce the value of the business at sale by as much as $4,470,000.

2. Recast your financial statements.
If time doesn't permit changing your accounting practices prospectively, his-

toric financial statements can be "recast" to show the "true" earnings of the business in prior years. This can be done at the time of sale by adding back adjustments to the earnings created by the prior use of aggressive tax accounting. A significant part (but probably not all) of the "reduced value" can be recaptured through this technique. Be aware, however, that buyers tend to discount the value of recast financial statements, because they require the buyer to rely on a story rather than on hard numbers.

Sellers who have to rely on recast financial statements rather than the actual statements (which preferably have been audited) will normally receive less for their businesses.

If you have to rely on recast statements to sell your business, you should be represented by an experienced professional in mergers and acquisitions who is knowledgeable in selling through the competitive auctioning process (see Rule 9). A skilled professional, adept at managing a competitive auctioning process can, in most instances, overcome the buyer's resistance to paying maximum prices for a business with recast financial statements.

3. Have your financial statements audited annually.
Businesses with audited financial statements normally receive the highest prices from buyers. Most entrepreneurs avoid having their financial statements audited. Usually they do so because of cost and because it can have an impact on the use of aggressive tax-accounting practices. But while audited statements may be unnecessary to the original owner of a business, they are extremely important and highly desired by potential buyers of the business.

Audited statements provide buyers with the highest level of confidence in the company's actual financial condition.

My advice is: if you want top dollar for your company, forget about the impact on taxes created by greater earnings. Two to three years before you sell, you need to maximize your reported book-earnings and make sure you have the statements audited. Do this, and I can promise that the increase you'll gain in the selling price of the business will be many times more than any extra taxes and auditing fees you would incur.

**HOW TO USE YOUR FINANCIAL
STATEMENTS TO MAXIMIZE VALUE**
- **Stop using aggressive accounting practices**
- **Recast your financial statements if necessary**
- **Have financial statements audited annually
  before beginning a sale**

Implement Managerial Practices That Strengthen Your Company Over the Long Term

If you have a successful business, then you must be a good business manager. Even so, some of your managerial practices may be just the opposite of what a buyer will be looking for. Things that you may be doing to maintain control over the direction of your business and to increase profits may or may not make the future of your company look bright to an outside buyer. There are several things you should do that are key to increasing the value placed on your business by a potential buyer.

1. Build a strong managerial team.
Of all the elements that should be in place in preparing a business for sale, building a strong managerial team may be the most important. Buyers always pay premiums for businesses that have strong managerial teams supporting the owner. Ideally, this team should include a manager capable of replacing the owner. In most privately held businesses, the owner is the dominant manager with, typically, a thin layer of senior management. Buyers become concerned about what will happen to the business if something should happen to the owner. Thus, businesses that lack depth in management are thought to present substantially greater risk of failure than businesses that retain good managerial teams after they are sold.

Many buyers will simply avoid considering a deal if a company has limited depth in management under a dominant owner/manager. Those who do consider the purchase will tend to discount the price they are willing to pay. When buyers go forward with a deal where they are wary about management, they will often protect their investment in the purchase by structuring the deal with a significant percentage of the consideration to be paid in the form of future payments like earnouts or non-compete payments. Structured deals are designed to ensure the seller's continued presence in management before the seller can obtain the entire purchase price. The less a buyer has to rely on the owner for the future success of the business, the higher the price the buyer will pay.

The sale of Ogden, Inc. is a perfect example of the tremendous value that can be achieved when the owner builds a great managerial team.

Ogden was a manufacturer of nationally branded plumbing products, whose owner/founder was 72 years old. This entrepreneur had an incredible ability to hire the right people for all of the critical positions in management of the business, then to delegate responsibility and authority to create an environment in which employees could demonstrate their managerial skills and excel. The managerial team was so good that it had already enabled the owner to remove himself from the daily management of the business. Buyers viewed the managerial team itself as having significant value. This perception made the company a highly prized acquisition for all of the buyers to whom I showed it.

The most important member of the managerial team was Linda, the company's president and chief operating officer. Linda was incredibly good at her job, and under her leadership the business had accumulated four straight record years of double-digit growth in sales and earnings. In developing a strategy for marketing the company, I decided to allow the buyers to focus on Linda and her managerial team and leave the owner out of the process of dealing with the buyers. The buyers were all attracted to Linda's managerial skills and accomplishments. It was clear to every buyer that after the sale, they could rely on Linda to continue to run the company.

Linda, not the owner, became my point person. Linda met with all buyer candidates who visited the company. She managed the buyers' tours of the plant, reviewed historical financials and future projections with the buyers, and presented the company's business plan that, most importantly, was her plan for the future of the business. It was clear to all buyers who visited that this was Linda's company and that she was responsible for its past success and could be counted on for its future performance.

Linda's absolute value to this transaction was enormous. Her most significant contribution was made at a meeting with the ultimate buyer. At that meeting, the president of the buyer's organization (a public company) asked her to talk about the company's future and the financial projections that had been presented to him in our marketing materials. The projections were quite aggressive, and he asked her what she really thought the business would do. In response, she looked the president in the eye and said "These are my projections, not the owner's, and I always exceed the projections that I make, so, if you buy this company, you can assume that I will meet or beat any projections that I commit to."

I saw a gleam in the buying president's eyes and knew at that point that the company was sold and that his company would pay whatever price was necessary to make the deal. They paid a huge price to buy Ogden, offering one-third more than the next highest bidder — more than the owner ever expected to receive. But what he didn't know was that 30 percent to 40 percent of that price existed solely because of Linda and her managerial team.

This story dramatically illustrates the value of a solid managerial team.

Building a great managerial team is the single most important area in which you can significantly increase the value of your business prior to its sale.

Start building your managerial team as soon as possible.

2. Develop a five-year business plan and implement it.

Your business plan will be presented as the strategic blueprint for the future of your business. It is the "story" that will be used to sell the business. (Selling the future of your business is critical and is the topic of Rule 11.) The "value," or credibility, attached to it will be greater if the business plan is being implemented at the time of sale.

WHAT TO ADDRESS IN YOUR
FIVE-YEAR BUSINESS PLAN
- **Operations**
- **Capital expenditures**
- **Financial history and future projections**
- **Information systems**
- **Sales and marketing**
- **Organization**
- **Products**
- **Development of products**
- **Competition**

The quality of your business plan will have a direct bearing on the value that the buyer places on the business.

Because the business plan is such a critical part of the selling process, securing outside assistance from a consultant or an advisor in mergers and acquisitions is an excellent idea.

3. Update facilities, equipment, and systems to state-of-the-art condition.

Buyers love companies with state-of-the-art facilities, equipment, and systems. They will pay big premiums to acquire them. Remember, the investment you make will pay multiple dividends at the time of sale. My experience is that businesses in state-of-the-art condition attract many more bidders and much higher prices than their outdated competitors.

4. Reduce dependence on a few large customers.

Buyers consider businesses that depend on one or two large customers to be extremely risky acquisitions. Most buyers I've encountered either avoid such companies entirely or make an offer that is substantially discounted to compensate for the risk. Business owners who depend on one or two large customers usually have a close relationship with the customer that has developed over a period of years. This relationship, whether real or imagined, creates a level of comfort in the mind of the owner which will never transfer to a buyer. Buyers are normally pessimistic about such relationships. They will be skeptical of the transferable value of the previous owner's relationship and will assume that there is a high probability of losing the major customer after the purchase.

Customer concentration is an extremely important issue in the sale of a business and is considered a major risk by buyers.

If you are planning to sell your business and want to sell for the highest price, immediately begin expanding your base of customers.

The ideal situation is to have no customer on whom you must depend for more than ten percent of your business, but in certain industries like the automotive industry, buyers recognize that this is impossible.

KEY MANAGERIAL PRACTICES
How you manage your company today determines how buyers view its future.

- **Build a strong team in management**
- **Develop a five-year business plan and implement it**
- **Update facilities, equipment, and systems to state-of-the-art condition**
- **Reduce dependence on a few large customers; expand the base of customers**

RULE 2

Make sure financial statements position your business in the most positive manner possible.

Financial statements are the main tools that buyers use to value a business. This is my experience, and I will continue to believe it to be true, no matter what else others may have to say on the subject. To sell your business for the highest price, you must understand how buyers look at financial statements. Your goal is to position your statements in the way that will be viewed most positively by the prospective buyers of your business.

Considerations in the Balance Sheet

1. Disclose assets that have market value that exceeds book value.

When you take your company to market, it is important that you disclose to all potential buyers the amount by which the market value of your assets exceeds their book value. Ideally, such disclosure should be substantiated by appraisals. The buyers' consideration of book value of assets compared to market value is especially important to owners of manufacturing companies. Manufacturers typically have invested millions of dollars in plant and equipment that has been depreciated below current fair market value. In such a situation, the net worth on the books of the company would be understated to the extent that the value of the real estate, machinery, and equipment on the books would be less than the value that these assets could be sold for.

There are three reasons why it is important for you to set forth to buyers the amount by which actual value of assets is in excess of their book value — all of which increase the buyer's motivation to buy and pay a higher price.

It improves the buyer's ability to finance the deal. Most buyers will be financing a significant part of the purchase price with a bank or similar asset-based lending institution. To the extent that the buyer can increase the value of assets upon which the acquisition loan is based, the amount that can be borrowed will increase, thereby increasing the amount of cash paid to the seller.

It decreases the buyer's perception of risk in the deal. Buyers view their initial economic risk in any deal as being the difference between the purchase price and the market value of assets purchased. Therefore, from the buyer's perspective, a reduction in risk occurs as the market value of assets acquired increases. Having a higher value for acquired assets often makes it easier for the buyer to do the deal, and in many instances results in an increase in the purchase price.

It brings the buyer great tax-benefits in the deal. Because of tax-benefits and reduced exposure, most buyers prefer to structure transactions as purchases of assets instead of purchases of stock. In purchases of assets, buyers want to reduce the amount of goodwill paid for, by allocating as much of the purchase price as possible to assets that can be written off more quickly. All acquired assets that have a market value in excess of their book value can be written up by the buyer to their market value and then depreciated or amortized over their allowable useful lives at the date of sale.

Maximize your selling price by always disclosing assets that have market values in excess of their book values, and always back up these increased values with an appraisal.

2. Disclose assets that have value but are not on the books.

Your company may have assets that are not disclosed on the books or financial statements but nevertheless have substantial value. Examples of such assets would be patents, trade names, lists of customers, proprietary software or systems, and proprietary tooling or molds that have been expensed. These are not the types of assets that banks will lend against. Disclosure of additional asset-value in this category will not facilitate additional financing for the buyer, but such disclosure is important to the buyer, especially if the transaction is to be structured as a sale of assets. In a transaction based on sale of assets, these assets would be given ascribed values and amortized or depreciated over a shorter period than is allowable for goodwill, thereby reducing allocations for goodwill and accelerating future benefits in income tax for the new owner.

It is important to keep in mind that even if the transaction is structured as a sale of stock, the disclosure of additional asset-values over those on the books is important, because it enables you to "recast" your balance sheet to reflect the real market value of your assets, *thus increasing the net worth of your company*. Every seller should keep in mind that "restated" net worth of a business is part of the equation that buyers use when they are determining the value of a business. Buyers tend to measure their risk by the premium paid over "restated" net worth. It is, therefore, incumbent upon every seller to do everything possible at the time of sale to "recast" the net worth of the company to higher levels.

3. Increase the amount of your company's liquid assets.

Buyers like companies with a high percentage of liquid assets. The more liquid the assets owned by a selling company, the more attractive the acquisition becomes to the buyer. This is because it is easier for the buyer to finance liquid assets (inventory and receivables). From a buyer's perspective, the more liquid the assets of a purchased business become, the less risk is involved in entering into the purchase. Keep in mind that a company with a high percentage of liquid assets will not necessarily sell for *more* than a company that is less liquid, but, it will be significantly *easier* to sell because it will be considered more desirable and easier to finance.

4. Increase value of inventory at the time of sale by adding back the LIFO (Last In First Out) inventory reserve.

When buyers investigate a company that is using the LIFO method for valuation of inventory, they always add back the reserve to determine the current value of the inventory they would be buying. Therefore, sellers should always "recast" the reserve back to increase the value of the inventory being sold. Remember that the buyer is really purchasing the FIFO (First In First Out) value, and the buyer's bank is making the loan on that value.

Adding back the LIFO reserve increases the net worth of the purchased company and theoretically reduces the purchaser's risk. This becomes a negotiating point for the seller. In reality, however, if the buyer were to sell the inventory and deplete the reserve, a large tax-liability would be incurred that would reduce the perceived value. This issue might arise in the negotiations, but a representative skilled in mergers and acquisitions should be able to negotiate around the potential tax-problem. I have never had a client who was unable to transfer future LIFO tax-problems to the buyer.

**POSITION YOUR BUSINESS WITH
FINANCIAL STATEMENTS THAT:**
- **Disclose assets that have market value that exceeds their book value**
- **Disclose assets that have value but are not on the books**
- **Increase your liquid assets**
- **Recast the LIFO reserve to increase the value of inventory**

Considerations of Company Debt

1. Reduce the amount of debt the buyer will have to assume.

When a buyer computes the value of your company, the amount of debt that will be assumed at the time of sale will be considered as an additional cost to the transaction. Buyers normally value companies using multiples of earnings on a debt-free basis. For example, at a six-times-multiple value, a business that earned a million dollars would be valued at $6 million. If the business has $2 million in debt, however, and that debt is going to be assumed by the buyer, the buyer will, dollar for dollar, reduce the purchase-price paid, so, the seller would receive $4 million cash for the business. The buyer would be paying $6 million for the business but only $4 million would be paid directly to the seller, and $2 million would be paid in assumed debt.

2. Operate the business prior to sale in a manner that generates cash.

You can maximize the cash you receive at the time of sale by using a number of methods to generate cash, and using the cash to reduce the debt-load of the business. For example a seller could, without causing a negative impact on the business, eliminate excess liquid assets, reduce unnecessary expenses, sell off old inventory, tighten collection procedures for receivables, and reduce capital expenditures. As long as the cash generated from these activities does not adversely affect profits, it would not affect the purchase price and would increase the cash to the seller at closing.

Considerations in the Profit and Loss Statement

1. Focus on before-tax earnings that reflect future growth in income.

Buyers use before-tax earnings to determine the selling price. In almost every transaction, the selling price as determined by the buyer is a multiple of the company's before-tax earnings. How high the multiple is computed will depend upon how secure the buyer feels about the future income of the business. Higher multiples are paid for businesses with secure, growing streams of income. Such businesses have patents or proprietary products, branded products, trademarks, or long-term contractual rights that provide the buyer with a level of confidence in the future stream of income from that business. Lower multiples are paid for companies with little or no proprietary nature to their business, such as contract manufacturers where the customer has more control than the manufacturer.

2. Make a forecast of growth that will have credibility with a buyer.

Buyers pay premiums for businesses that are growing. Every company being sold prepares a forecast for future sales and profits, but I have yet to come across a business for sale that is forecasting flat or decreasing sales and profits. Everyone forecasts growth. Buyers know this, and so they are usually skeptical of forecasts.

Forecasted growth gains credibility only when it is compared to current and historical growth. For example, a company that has been growing at a rate of 20 percent per year for the last five years could forecast continued growth at that rate and such a forecast would have credibility. It would be difficult, however, to find credibility in the same forecast for a company where sales had been flat for the last three years.

Buyers pay big premiums for growing companies, and they measure future growth by looking at current and historical growth. Thus, to sell for the highest price, you must sell when your business is in a period of growth.

Only at that time can you paint a credible scenario for continued growth that will command a premium selling price. Remember, the reason to sell while you are growing rapidly is that, by waiting, you take the risk that the premium will drop or disappear entirely should the company's growth stop or slow down.

Considerations of Capital Expenditures

When preparing your business for sale, it is important to develop and implement a consistent program for capital expenditures. In some cases business owners, especially those with Sub-Chapter S corporations, will defer needed capital expenditures and milk the company, pulling all the money they can out of the business, prior to putting it on the market. The business owner's theory is that the buyer will invest in the business and make needed capital expenditures. This is a shortsighted approach to the sale that almost always makes the business less attractive to buyers and results in a lower price for the seller. When sellers cut back on capital expenditures needed to facilitate growth of the business, buyers will normally plan to reinstate those cutbacks after the sale. In determining business value, however, they will, in almost every case, take a conservative approach and assume that they will need to spend more money than the seller would have spent to achieve the desired result. Such additional forecasted spending (over and above the amount needed if the seller had been diligent in making capital expenditures) will be treated by the buyer as a direct reduction in the purchase price.

> **Sellers who, over a period of time, cut back on needed capital expenditures will usually have to accept a lower price for their business.**

Recasting Financial Statements

All buyers are aware that a number of entrepreneurs will understate their profits on the books in order to save taxes. They also know that many sellers take out excessive salaries and "perks" that will not exist after sale. Nevertheless, buyers always attempt to negotiate the sale price on the basis of booked profits. This is a common tactic employed by buyers in an attempt to reduce the purchase price. The best response to the buyer looking at booked earnings is for the seller to use "recasting." In recasting, the seller modifies the current and historical financial statements on the books of the business to reflect the true earnings of the business. Sellers should only use recast statements as a basis for negotiations, and use them only when the financial statements on the books understate the true earnings. Financial statements on the books that present the true value of the business should not be recast.

TYPICAL ADJUSTMENTS IN
RECAST FINANCIAL STATEMENTS

Add back to income on the books:

1. **Excessive salaries and expenses paid to the owner.**
   Determine the add-back by comparing *the owner's pay to the cost of a professional manager.*

2. **All "family" expenses that would be eliminated after the sale.**
   Examples of such adjustments would be on-staff family members eliminated and not replaced after the sale.

3. **All extraordinary and unusual charges, costs, and write-downs in order to show the business's normal and expected profitability.**
   Examples of such items would be unusual legal fees and settlements; costs associated with plant-closings and startups; costs associated with discontinued operations and product-lines; costs of environmental clean-up and unusual or extraordinary costs incurred to comply with other regulatory agencies; and costs associated with unpredictable problems such as strikes, floods, and fires.

4. **The additional income that would have been reported for all items that should have been capitalized but instead were expensed.**

5. **All costs and expenses that would no longer be applicable in the hands of a new owner.**
   Examples of such costs would be unusually generous plans for bonuses and "perks," costs of outside consultants and advisors, directors' fees, excess expenses for attending conventions, costs of company-owned condominiums, and other such items.

6. **All adjustments that resulted in reducing inventory below its real value in order to save taxes.**

Properly recasting financial statements is a complicated process and should be completed with the help of an experienced professional.

My experience with recasting is that sellers should be aggressive but realistic in developing their recast adjustments. For consistency, make sure that all statements of income for prior years that are part of the financial presentation given to prospective buyers are recast.

**MAKE SURE FINANCIAL STATEMENTS
POSITION YOU MOST POSITIVELY**

Balance sheet
>   1. Disclose market values that exceed book values
>   2. Disclose valued assets not now on the books
>   3. Increase liquid assets
>   4. Use LIFO-reserve to increase inventory at sale

Company debt
>   1. Reduce debt to be assumed
>   2. Generate cash prior to sale

Profit-and-loss statement
>   1. Focus on before-tax earnings reflecting future
>   growth in income
>   2. Forecast growth credibly

Capital expenditures

Recast financial statements

RULE 3

Don't worry about income taxes. Do everything you can to maximize earnings.

Although this has been mentioned already, it's important enough to be a rule all by itself — *you must maximize the earnings of your business in order to get the most money possible.* Most buyers value businesses they want to purchase by using multiples of earnings before interest and taxes (EBIT). Disregard anything you have heard to the contrary.

As previously stated, the primary method used by buyers to value a business is to examine its historical and projected financial statements. The level of credibility a buyer attaches to these financial statements has a direct impact on pricing. The greater the credibility a buyer can attribute to your statements, the higher the price the buyer will be willing to pay for the business. Therefore, if you want to maximize the value of your company, do everything possible to add credibility to your financial presentation, even if it doesn't feel good while you're doing it.

This means you must forget about any extraordinary methods that you customarily employ to save taxes. The sooner you begin to do this, the better, because your increased earnings will show on your historical financial statements, lending credibility to your future projections for growth. Once your business is sold, taxes on future earnings will be the problem of the new owner. Meanwhile, your goal is to increase reported earnings, and you accomplish this by controlling your natural inclination to save taxes and avoid maximizing the income of the business as reported on the books.

A good way to change your perspective once you have committed to becoming a seller is to operate your business from a financial standpoint as though you were a public company. Public companies strive to maximize reported earnings per share.

TO MAXIMIZE REPORTED EARNINGS:
- **Capitalize everything you can**
- **Make sure *all* the income is on the books**
- **Eliminate excessive salaries, write-offs, reserves, and "perks" (special fringe benefits to the owner)**
- **Bring these amounts back into income**

I know it is difficult to change old habits, but the following example will explain why it makes sense.

Like many owners of businesses, Bill Morgan, the owner of XY Com Corporation, a very successful manufacturer of industrial controls, believed in the use of aggressive accounting tactics to reduce federal income taxes. Every year he wrote off or expensed everything he could. In 1997 Bill's business did $25 million in sales and had a book EBIT of $3 million. The EBIT for 1997 was really $4.5 million, but Bill had been very aggressive in deciding that the $1.5 million he spent for modernization of and improvements to the plant should be expensed instead of being capitalized, thereby reducing his EBIT from $4.5 to $3 million.

In January of 1998, Bill decided to sell the business. At that time his mergers-and-acquisitions advisor told him that businesses like his, in his industry, with good prospects, were selling for seven times the prior year's EBIT. Bill's business was worth $21 million. Bill then explained that the $3 million earnings reported on the books were not the real numbers. The business earned $4.5 million and should be worth at least $31.5 million. Upon examination of the $1.5 million write-off, Bill's M&A advisor agreed that these expenses probably should have been capitalized. On the other hand, a legitimate argument could be made that some or all of these expenditures were properly expensed. Bill and his M&A advisor decided to treat the $1.5 million write-off as an add-back to earnings for 1997 when presenting restated statements of historical income to potential buyers. They realized that many potential buyers, however, could conclude that the real earnings of the business were, indeed, the $3 million reported. A legitimate argument could be made to support the expenses.

Bill's experience discloses that buyers will not always give you credit for restated adjustments of earnings for the prior years. If Bill had capitalized the $1.5 million and his auditors had approved this treatment, it would be very unlikely that any buyer would ever raise the issue of the potential for expensing these costs. If the capitalized treatment had already been on the books, this business would almost certainly have been valued by buyers on the basis of a multiple of $4.5 million of earnings for 1997 instead of $3 million.

Restated earnings are never worth as much as earnings reported on the books.

RULE 4

Don't milk the net worth out of your business prior to sale.

Many owners of privately held companies make Sub-Chapter S elections for income tax purposes that allow them to take all of the cash out of the company annually, leaving the business with insufficient capital to provide for future growth. If you are a Sub-Chapter S corporation, it is important for you to understand that a history of stripping capital out of your business through Sub-Chapter S distributions to shareholders can result in a reduction of business value when you decide to sell. To maximize business value in today's mergers-and-acquisitions market, you must leave capital in the company. Use this capital to invest in a new plant, machinery, equipment, products, and so on. Such investments will pay big dividends when buyers value the business. Remember, buyers are purchasing the future, so make it look as good as you can.

> **You are not going to be able to take all the money out of your business and still receive the highest value when you try to sell it.**

RULE 5

Do not sell your business only when you are ready. Sell when market conditions are peaking and the future looks the brightest.

You may be reading this book because you have already made a decision that now is the best time for you to sell your business. But is this the optimal time to proceed? *The best time to sell is not just when you are ready, but when business and market conditions are strong and its value is optimum.* This is the key to maximizing value when your business is sold, and this requires pre-sale planning.

This point can't be overemphasized. Most entrepreneurs have a poor sense of timing when it comes to selling their business. Entrepreneurs usually base their decision to sell on personal reasons, and therefore they sell *when they are ready,* not when the business and the market are ready. The result is that only the lucky entrepreneurs who happen to be ready to sell during peak market conditions maximize value. A poorly timed sale usually means you will leave a lot of money on the table.

If you want to sell for the highest price, you should be pragmatic as you approach the idea of a sale, treating the business as if it were an economic investment like a stock, bond, or piece of real estate. You should be an opportunist, marketing the business when its future looks the brightest. If that coincides with a strong market in mergers and acquisitions, so much the better.

The most important aspect affecting value is that you are selling the future. Never lose sight of this fact. *Sell when the future of the business is at its peak.*

As the owner of a business, you are aware that owning a business is not like owning an annuity or a government bond. There are many risks you must take and factors beyond your control that can negatively impact your business and its value. For example, you could lose a major customer or have unanticipated problems dealing with environmental agencies, unions, regulatory agencies, or foreign competition.

I can think of three Detroit-based businesses in automotive supply that I dealt with in the mid-1980s, which should have been sold at that time. Each of these businesses was worth between $5 and $10 million. I advised each of the owners on numerous occasions that conditions in the mid-1980s made this the absolute best time ever to sell their companies. Their earnings were strong, the automotive sector was strong, and M&A market values were at an all-time high. But, none of these owners was ready to sell. They all believed that a business was like an annuity or a bond that they could own for as long as they wanted, and when they were ready to sell, they would get their price.

Unfortunately, they neglected to take into account the element of risk. The condition of the automotive market began to decline in the late 1980s and deteriorated in the recession of the 1990s. Furthermore, in the same time period, their customers decided to reduce their number of vendors. To make a long story short, all three of these companies with values of $5 to $10 million in the 1980s are now out of business, casualties of cyclical decline and vendor-consolidation in the automotive sector.

The moral of this story is simple. Be cognizant of market and business conditions. If these conditions peak at the same time, and if you are going to be a seller, that's the time to sell. Waiting until you are ready, for personal reasons, could create risks that reduce the future value of the business.

My experience with a company in technology is an excellent example of the importance of timing to a sale.

A rapidly growing distributor of high-capacity memory storage devices for computers, EZ Tech had been in business for seven years and was growing at the rate of 30 percent to 40 percent annually. It was a niche player, in that it had a very knowledgeable sales staff, most of whom were engineers specializing in selling this leading-edge technology. The products they sold were always in short supply and, in many cases, were being allocated by the manufacturers. Because EZ Tech was a specialist in these kinds of products, however, its suppliers always provided it with sizeable quota allotments. This resulted in sales at higher margins because of the lack of competitive pressure on price.

My clients, who were in their 30s, were riding a business that was like a rocket ship. They were also farsighted enough to see changes in the market that would impact their business. They knew their suppliers were all considering significant plant-expansions, which would ultimately result in overcapacity in the industry. This, in turn, would cause intensified competition and would lower margins for distributors like themselves.

The owners of EZ Tech decided to sell while their business was peaking and its future looked bright. Market conditions had never been better, and they did not want to take the risk of the negative impact on the market that would be caused by overcapacity at their vendors. The firm was sold to a large New York Stock Exchange company at the absolute highest value obtainable. Two years after the sale, the company's vendors began to open their new plants. Within six months, EZ Tech's gross margins began to deteriorate dramatically.

If my clients had held the business for two more years and then tried to sell it, its value would have been 50 percent of what they received.

THE BEST TIME TO SELL IS:
- **When performance of the business is peaking**
- **When the future of the business looks the brightest**
- **When the mergers-and-acquisitions market is strong**

RULE 6

Select the right mergers-and-acquisitions advisor to represent your company.

Once you have begun the process of preparing your business for sale, you will need to determine what is the right time to begin working with an expert. You may want to bring someone in at an early stage of the process to help you prepare and analyze the market for your company. But whatever you do, make sure you find a mergers-and-acquisitions advisor who is right for your company. Having the wrong M&A advisor could be worse than having none at all. Rule six gives you some important guidelines to follow.

Characteristics of a Good M&A Advisor

1. Should have broad experience in selling private companies.
Regardless of an advisor's track record in selling large, publicly held companies, there is simply no substitute for experience gained from selling a broad variety of private businesses. Large public companies have established market values, and there is much less flexibility in structuring transactions. The sale of a private company, on the other hand, requires careful consideration of technical issues such as taxes, earnouts, installment notes, escrows, contracts with management, and seller-retained equity.

Traditionally, transactions representing values in the range of $5 million to $50 million have had low priority among large investment banking firms. If your transaction is within that range, look for firms dedicated to the sale of private businesses in that price range. Look for advisors with extensive backgrounds in working with private companies to structure customized transactions that meet the individual needs of owners of private businesses.

2. Should be with a firm where you will get attention from senior level personnel.

Agree to work only with a firm that guarantees to dedicate a senior investment banker to your sale. Make it clear that you want this senior level person to work closely with you through all phases of your transaction and to represent you exclusively in the marketplace. If you deal with a large investment bank and the sale of your business is going to be smaller than a $50 million valuation, it is likely that the investment bank will want to assign junior staff members to your account. Therefore, if you cannot obtain the commitment of attention from personnel at the senior level, find another firm.

3. Should be available to you throughout the transaction.

Before signing on with a firm, you want to be assured that the team assigned to your company will work with you from start to finish. The investment bankers you meet initially should be the ones with whom you will work. There should be no switching later. You do not want to waste time educating new members of their team about your business and personal objectives. You want to be assured that the investment bankers you worked with as they solicited your business will not be diverted from you to larger transactions.

Here is an example of what can happen if you don't have an agreement on these points up front:

> George Moore, the owner of Detroit Plastics, decided to sell his business, which produced automotive plastic components. George believed his business was worth $35 million. He consulted his attorney and asked for recommendations for M&A advisors to manage the sales process. The attorney recommended three firms for George to interview — an M&A "boutique" firm in Detroit, a large New York investment banking firm, and my firm.

When I made my presentation, I asked with whom I was competing. I was told that the New York investment banking firm had brought in one of its senior managing directors to pitch the assignment. This individual was well known on Wall Street and had completed billions of dollars in investment deals. Upon hearing this, I warned George that the initial presentation of a big New York firm can be overwhelming, considering the experience of their managing directors, but that these firms do not normally take on smaller assignments — they typically want assignments valued at $100 million or more. Furthermore, the deals on which managing directors work are valued at $200 million or more, with success fees of at least $2 to $3 million. For George's transaction, the fee would probably have been $700,000. Thus, if they did decide to take on an assignment of this size, they would assign it to an associate at a junior level who would have less experience, and the managing director who pitched the assignment would move on to larger projects.

Although I really wanted the deal, I told George that if he preferred the New York firm, he should go ahead and sign with them if the managing director from the New York firm would commit to work the transaction. I also advised him to obtain a written commitment stating that the managing director who pitched the deal would manage his project and would be solely responsible for it. George disregarded the second half of my advice and signed with the New York firm. I hate to say "I told you so," but as soon as the letter of engagement was signed, the accomplished managing director disappeared, and the project was assigned to less experienced employees at the junior level. These employees lacked the knowledge and experience necessary to consummate a transaction at the price George desired.

Ultimately, the New York firm failed to satisfy George's needs. He became disenchanted with the caliber of the people assigned to his project and developed negative feelings about the firm. George terminated the engagement letter with the New York firm and was so disillusioned by the process that he decided to wait a few years before he would attempt to sell again. Three years later, I sold Detroit Plastics, and George and I remain good friends, seeing each other two to three times a year.

What To Expect From Your M&A Advisor

1. Demand sensitivity to your selling objectives.
In order to negotiate the deal *you want,* it is critical that your investment banker/advisor understand *your business* and *your selling objectives.* How

long do you want to continue working in your business? Do you want to cash out completely, or stay on as a partner and build your business toward another payday for yourself and your family?

The advisor can also help you to refine your selling objectives. Putting a price on your business is only one aspect of negotiating its sale. The advisor must also take the time to understand exactly how and when you desire to be compensated. Only after reaching such an understanding can the advisor structure the transaction to obtain the optimal result. For example, certain forms of employment contracts, notes, earnouts, and payment in stock rather than cash can help to maximize a seller's priorities for achieving the best price consistent with goals in liquidity and security.

Look for investment bankers/advisors who have a great deal of experience in successfully understanding and representing the selling objectives of owners of private businesses. No two deals ever go exactly the same way. Thus, an advisor who can draw on closely related experience when problems and opportunities present themselves is vitally important.

2. Demand and maintain confidentiality.
Your advisor should respect the level of confidentiality that you demand and should be able to adjust sales strategies accordingly. Unauthorized leaks of your prospective sale can cause personal and business embarrassment, damage present and future relations for your company, and jeopardize the sale itself. Of course, no advisor can provide an ironclad solution to this issue, because the need to approach outside buyers presents difficulties. In general, the advisor who knows how to profile the buyer with the greatest precision possible, and thereby ensure having the smallest group of qualified, high-likelihood potential buyers from the outset, has the best shot at maintaining confidentiality. This selectivity, coupled with an aggressive program to achieve confidentiality with each potential buyer contacted (including various confidentiality agreements), provides a high degree of assurance that the confidentiality of the transaction will be secure. Another factor is timing. The faster the selling process takes place, the better your chances are of maintaining confidentiality.

3. Look for an advisor with significant contacts among buyers and who has back-up support.

Your advisor should be able to draw quickly upon extensive domestic and foreign contacts with buyers and resources in backup support when selling your company. The broader the spectrum of potential buyers, the more likelihood there is of obtaining a premium price. Your investment banker should be able to effect introductions quickly and to pin down meetings with appropriately profiled buyers. Ready access to foreign buyers who are aggressively seeking investment opportunities is also a factor. Most full-service firms will be able to draw on an extensive array of support services in order to identify the best group of buyers for your business. These support services include a network of employees, a database developed over many years that contains thousands of active individual and corporate buyers, and strong, long-term relationships with other investment banks and buyers in the U.S., Europe, and Asia.

4. Factor cost-effectiveness into your decision.

In making your ultimate decision on whom to hire as your M&A consultant, you have to consider fees just as you would with any other business transaction. How heavily you weigh this factor against the others discussed here will be your call. Here are some things to keep in mind about fees:

- ◆ Fees should be cost-effective, resulting in a successful transaction at the desired price within a reasonable period of time.
- ◆ Most securities firms and business brokers charge an up-front, non-refundable retainer supplemented by another fee on closing. The up-front retainer helps defray the significant commitment made to representing your company properly.
- ◆ Almost all of the consideration paid to an investment banker/advisor is a "success fee" payable *only* upon the completion of the transaction. This approach assures you that your advisor is properly motivated to carry the transaction all the way through to a closing.
- ◆ In most cases, advisors' out-of-pocket expenses, such as travel, legal fees, computer time, and so forth, are reimbursed in addition to the "success fee" regardless of completion of the transaction. ∽

YOUR M&A ADVISOR SHOULD OFFER YOU:
- Broad experience in selling private companies
- Attention from personnel at the senior level
- Personal dedication of a senior representative
  throughout the transaction
- Sensitivity to your selling objectives
- Confidentiality
- Significant contacts among buyers, and backup
  support
- Cost-effective fees for handling the transaction

PART II

Rules to Follow
DURING
the Sales Process

RULE 7

Do not try to sell the business yourself.

Repeat: *Do not try to sell the business yourself.* This advice cannot be stated emphatically enough. Of all the things that can prevent you from getting the most out the sale, attempting to sell your own business ranks as number one. Why? You can give some answers to this yourself, on the basis of what you read in Part I. But here, in a nutshell, are the key reasons.

1. Selling a business for the highest price is a time-consuming (nine to twelve months or longer), complicated process that requires the knowledge and experience of a professional.
Here is a list of the areas of knowledge needed to maximize the value of your sale:

- ◆ Accounting
- ◆ Finance
- ◆ Law
- ◆ Purchase-and-sale agreements
- ◆ Environmental and regulatory issues
- ◆ Financing of working capital and acquisitions
- ◆ Market conditions in mergers and acquisitions
- ◆ Market conditions in your industry
- ◆ Strategic goals of buyers and criteria used by buyer for acquisitions

The person who sells your company with knowledge of these key areas will know the value of current transactions and the prices being paid for companies similar to yours. More importantly, he or she will also possess the experience and knowledge required to position and market your company and the ability to negotiate complicated mergers-and-acquisitions deals to command the highest selling price on terms acceptable to you. To sell a company successfully using a multi-buyer auction (see Rule 8), a large group of potential buyers (including foreign buyers) must be found and an interest must be developed within this group. Only a professional experienced in mergers and acquisitions will have all of the required expertise and resources to pull this off.

2. Maximum selling prices are always generated when the owner's time is spent managing the business instead of managing its sale.

Owners who try to sell their own businesses are getting themselves involved in a complicated process in which they have no experience and which takes valuable time away from the management of their companies. Reduced attention to the management of the business can have a negative impact on profitability and can actually *reduce* the value of your company. An owner who continues to spend full time running the business in order to *maximize* profits will increase the value of the business during the sale process.

3. It is "penny-wise and dollar-foolish" to attempt to sell your business yourself when you only want to save the fee you would have to pay a professional intermediary.

My experience is that even if owners are successful in handling their own sale, they will normally sell for substantially less than a professional organization would be able to get for the business. This disparity in pricing occurs because business owners are unable to access a large number of potential buyers, and they do not sell through a competitive auctioning process that maximizes value.

The case of Precision Industrial is a good example of what can happen when an owner tries to sell his business himself.

Precision Industrial was a Cleveland-area manufacturer of precision component parts for the automotive, aerospace, and medical device industries. The company, with $50 million in sales, was considered to be a premier supplier to its customer base. Bill, the owner, who was in his mid-fifties, was not thinking of selling until he was approached by Sam, a social acquaintance, who also happened to be president of a larger player in the industry. Because of this social relationship, Bill felt comfortable discussing a possible sale with Sam. Sam offered Bill an all-cash deal of $49 million or 6.5 times the EBIT (earnings before interest and taxes) for Precision's prior year. Bill thought this was a very good deal, but he was basing his judgment on a very limited amount of information. He knew that other companies in his industry had been sold for 5.5 to 6 times EBIT, but he didn't know market conditions or who the other buyers were, nor what they would pay.

Fortunately for Bill, he took the proposed deal to his attorney, who happened to be skilled in mergers and acquisitions. The attorney told Bill that while it looked like a good deal, he should keep in mind that he had spent 25 years building his business, that he would sell it only once, and that he should obtain the best possible price when he sold it. The attorney recommended that Bill consult with a mergers-and-acquisitions specialist to gauge market conditions and value, before he moved ahead with the proposed deal.

The attorney introduced Bill to me. After assessing the value of his business, I told Bill that market conditions were very dynamic and favored sellers. He had a great business that was strategically positioned in his industry, and because of that there would be dozens of buyers who would actively bid. In addition, there were a number of foreign buyers who would pay dearly for his business, because it would be a great vehicle for them to enter the large U.S. market and access his blue-chip customer-base. My assessment was that the market would pay a lot more than 6.5 times EBIT, and I suggested that the business should be marketed to a large number of strategic buyers, including the buyer he was currently dealing with, through a competitive auctioning process. I explained that the buyer who had made him an offer had a strategic interest in Precision, and this interest would not be diminished if we involved other potential buyers in the process. At the very minimum, the process would make that buyer increase its bid.

Bill saw the advantages of using the process I described and, in the end, I sold Precision to a large German company that wanted to enter the U.S. market and access Bill's blue-chip customer-base. The German company paid nine times EBIT, or $67.5 million. This was $18.5 million more than Bill would have received had he sold the company himself. By the way, I should point out that the process caused the original potential buyer to increase its bid by $10 million over the original offer of $49 million.

Contacting a number of buyers in a competitive auctioning process always develops values that more than justify the fee you pay to the intermediary who is handling the process.

Throughout this book I advise the reader to use a professional mergers-and-acquisitions advisor when you sell your business. A review of the complications involved in the strategies and implementation of the sale process clearly illustrates why competent help is needed. The following chart illustrates exactly why the business owner should always hire a competent mergers-and-acquisitions advisor to manage the sale.

Advantages of Using a Professional Mergers-and-Acquisitions Advisor	
OWNER HANDLES SALE	**OWNER RETAINS PROFESSIONAL ADVISOR**
Owner sells when ready, usually for personal reasons.	Advisor has the owner sell when the timing and value are optimum.
Selling price is what owner thinks is fair — usually below market value, due to lack of competitive buyers.	Advisor sells for the highest price the market will pay and uses competitve selling processes.
Owner deals with one buyer.	Advisor deals with multiple buyers and uses an auctioning process that involves a large universe of buyers.
Owner seldom deals with foreign buyers.	Advisor deals with numerous foreign buyers to bid up the price.
Owner sells for the best deal perceived as obtainable, but the price may be limited because the owner deals with only one or two buyers.	Advisor sells for the highest price guaranteed by a competitive selling process.
Owner's management of the sale interferes with their ability to operate the business.	Advisor manages the sale so the owner can continue to run the business.
Owner sells to save advisor's fees, but sells for a lower price and loses much more in value than would be saved in fees.	Prices generated by advisors in a competitive auctioning process will more than justify the fees paid.
Owner is an expert in running the business but an amateur in handling the sale.	Advisor is an experienced M&A professional whose business is selling companies.

RULE 8

Never state an asking price for the business.

Don't decide your selling price in advance. That may sound like strange advice, but here's why: *Deciding on an asking price for the business is not in the seller's best interest, because it usually results in limiting the selling price to the asking price.* This is another reason why it's important to work with a professional who has experience in employing this tactic, which requires considerable skill. Why is this so important? Because very often buyers see additional value in the seller's business. The only way to extract this value is through a competitive auctioning process with no asking price. Placing an asking price on the business eliminates most of the value of a competitive selling process (see Rule 9). If you had to use one word to describe it — it's an *auction*.

> **The competitive selling process lets the market drive the value to its highest possible level.**

RULE 9

Sell through a competitive auctioning process involving multiple buyers.

There's an easy way to come to an appreciation of not placing a price on your business but instead using the auctioning process. Think of your business as a valuable Picasso painting that you want to sell. You surely would have no problem on your own in finding a number of buyers who would be interested in purchasing this work of art. Nevertheless, you would never even consider trying to sell it yourself. Instead, you would take the painting to one of the world's top art-auction houses, because you know that the auctioning process itself creates prices so high that they more than justify the auctioneer's fee. So why wouldn't that same rationale be equally applicable to the selling of a business?

Managing the auctioning process takes considerable skill and experience, however. When you select a mergers-and-acquisitions advisor, you must be sure the advisor has these skills. Checking with prior clients is one way to verify this. For your own knowledge, there are several key reasons to use the auctioning process:

1. Multiple buyers create competition, and competition is the principal lever that raises the price.
This principle is the same as that applied by business owners when they are sourcing a vendor for a key component. Placing the component out for bid with a number of vendors who bid against one another to obtain the busi-

ness is the way to get the lowest and best price. The only difference in a sale situation is that bidding is used to drive the price up.

2. The auctioning process creates substantial leverage for the seller while putting the buyer in a substantially weaker position.

The buyer loses control and flexibility due to being bound by the rules of the auctioning process. Those rules are set by the seller.

3. Dealing with multiple buyers provides you with choices about who gets your company.

While price is of paramount importance to any seller, I find that my clients seldom turn their businesses over to a buyer with whom they have poor personal chemistry. If you are like most sellers, you want to have a choice of buyers and will ultimately choose a buyer that makes you feel comfortable. This is part of knowing that you are making the right decision about who gets your company.

4. Dealing with multiple buyers provides the seller with back-up buyers — a form of insurance that the deal will close.

When a deal falls through, usually it is killed because the buyer is unable to finalize it and pulls out. If you are dealing with a single buyer, and that buyer pulls out, you must start the selling process all over again. With multiple buyers, your advisor will be able to keep buyers number two and three in place until the deal closes. If the deal with your first choice falls through, you can quickly replace buyer number one with buyer number two and keep the action moving forward.

Dealing with multiple buyers gives the seller tremendous leverage in negotiating and closing the deal.

Superior deals always result when buyers know they have competition. Competition favorably affects all aspects of the deal, including price, structure, and terms. It also provides the seller's attorney with leverage in negotiating with the buyer's attorney on the contract.

RULE 10

Expand your search for buyers beyond your competitors and known synergistic buyers.

While it is only natural to look within the realm of your own industry when planning to sell your business, a good M&A person can expand your horizons and, by doing so, command a higher price for your business. Buyers in unrelated businesses tend to pay the highest prices, because their strategic plans have made such acquisitions necessary to complement their long-term strategic goals. My experience with selling more than 75 companies is that 75 percent of them were purchased by buyers who were not competitors and were not synergistically related to the seller's business. An illustration is a company I sold in 1989.

Michigan Engineering, a Detroit-based tool-and-die manufacturer, was acquired by a $500 million Japanese public company that was not in the tool-and-die business or in any other related business. Normally they wouldn't have been on anyone's list of buyers for this deal, but by expanding my search for a buyer to Japan, I was able to locate this company. I found out that they had a strategic plan to enter the tool-and-die industry in the United States in order to support their relationship as a vendor to Toyota and Honda. They paid a substantial premium to purchase Michigan Engineering (double the offers of all U.S. buyers) to make their first acquisition in the U.S. tool-and-die industry.

Foreign buyers consistently pay a premium for their first acquisition in a given industry in the U.S.

What about looking at deals with synergistic buyers and players in your industry who have offered to purchase your business in the past? In this case, it can be even more important to expand your network of buyers, because these companies may have altered their corporate goals by the time you're ready to sell, and they may be less interested or no longer interested in a deal.

A perfect example of this situation is a transaction I handled in 1992 for Diamond Distribution, a large Midwest-based food-distributing company. Two years before the sale, the two largest companies in the food-distributing industry approached the owner. Both of them offered to buy Diamond, but at that time the owner was not ready to sell. A year later, the owner changed his mind about selling and hired me to represent him. He believed that the natural buyer would be one of these two companies.

When I took Diamond into the market, however, neither of these players in that industry was interested in pursuing Diamond. Both were heavily involved in other acquisitions. Fortunately, I did not need the participation of these two industry players to sell the company, having greatly expanded my universe of buyers to include a number of financial buyers, one of which stepped up to pay a very high price in order to get the deal and create a platform for further consolidation.

Are you getting the picture? *Don't rely on what you know or what you think you know about where to find a good buyer for your company.* If you don't expand your universe of buyers, you will often find that the "slam dunk" buyer you counted on may be involved in other projects, or for other reasons may choose not to pursue the deal. Without an expanded base of buyers, you have no deal.

When you expand your universe of buyers, always include a number of foreign and financial buyers. Make sure that your mergers-and-acquisitions advisor has access to these buyers.

RULE 11

Sell the future, not the past.

In Part I, we talked about selling your company's future. Now let's look at it from another angle. First, we know that past and current earnings of the business belong to the seller. The buyer is purchasing the future income-stream of the business. While buyers do understand that they are buying the business's future income-stream, they believe that the best indication of future earnings is found in an examination of the historical base of earnings for the business. If you want to *maximize* your selling price you must take every conceivable step to maximize historical growth of profits and sales *before you sell*.

1. A solid history of profitability and growth gives credibility to pricing of the company based upon projections of profitability and growth for the future.

Selling the future of a business works in a way similar to the way a stockbroker sells a customer a new stock. The broker tells the customer a story about the company and presents a rationale for why the customer should believe that company will achieve significant growth in earnings in the future. If you buy the stock, you buy it for its projected future earnings. Buyers of businesses have a similar objective.

The strategy of selling the future income-stream of the business transfers risk to the buyer.

When you sell the future, the buyer is paying a premium for future earnings, but *these earnings may never materialize.* The buyer is *assuming the risk* that those earnings will materialize and is paying the seller in advance for earnings that may never be realized. Selling the future is an important technique, because it enables the seller to receive value for future earnings regardless of whether these earnings actually occur. To maximize value by selling the future, you should make sure that the mergers-and-acquisitions advisor you retain has experience in using this technique.

The following example shows how selling the future works.

Automotive Supplier Selling the Future						
	Historical			Year of Sale	Projections Used in the Sales Process		
	1986	1987	1988	1989	1990	1991	1992
Sales	10,000	11,500	13,000	15,000	18,000	21,000	25,000
Profit	1,000	1,150	1,300	1,500	1,800	2,100	2,500

Actual Results				
	1989	1990	1991	1992
Sales	15,000	16,000	14,000	11,500
Profits	1,500	1,300	700	(500)

In this case, the seller effectively used the technique of selling the future and was paid for earnings that never materialized. The seller was able to obtain a premium price on the basis of projected future earnings because the past and current track record of the business was one of solid growth in sales and profits. The 1989 purchase price was predicated on the value of future growth in earnings that never materialized due to an unforeseen downturn in the automotive sector in the 1990-92 period. If the seller had not sold the business in 1989, he would have incurred substantially decreased earnings and a significant reduction in the worth of the business.

2. A business plan sells the future.

If you want to sell the future, you must develop a long-term business plan for your company. A well thought out business plan is synonymous to the story the broker told you when he wanted to sell you a new stock. The business plan is the roadmap you will show to potential buyers that discloses how the business will grow and prosper under new ownership. If you are unable to develop such a plan on your own, seek help from outside consultants or a competent mergers-and-acquisitions advisor who is capable of providing such assistance.

MAKE SURE YOUR BUSINESS PLAN ADDRESSES:
- **Operations**
- **Capital expenditures**
- **Financial history and future projections**
- **Information systems**
- **Sales and marketing**
- **Organization**
- **Products and product development**
- **Competition**

Your business plan is the strategic blueprint for the next five years, and it is the "story" that will be used to sell your company. If the story has sizzle, it will be reflected in the number of buyers bidding on the business and the aggressiveness in their bids.

RULE 12

Educate yourself on the types of buyers in the market and on how to find them.

Knowledge of buyers is critical to success. While your mergers-and-acquisitions advisor will be the expert, the background knowledge given here is necessary in order for you to make the right decisions about who handles your sale and, ultimately, who buys your company.

1. Understand the differences in types of buyers.

Buyers fall into two broad categories that greatly affect how they acquire. The first category is *strategic* or *industry* buyers who acquire because a company falls within their strategic operating plan. An example of a strategic acquisition would be Compaq's acquisition of Digital Equipment Corporation. A strategic target probably has an attractive line of products, base of customers, or network for distribution that the buyer wishes to own. The second category is *financial* buyers who acquire businesses as an investment. An example of an acquisition by a financial buyer would be the purchase by KKR of RJR Nabisco. Typically backed by pension funds, insurance companies, or individuals with high net worth, financial buyers wish to generate attractive returns by investing in companies of good quality, growing them, and selling them in five to seven years for a substantial profit.

Either type of buyer may be an appropriate partner, depending on your selling objective. Strategic buyers are more likely to generate fundamental improvements in the business such as increased sales or a better network of distribution, since those are the driving reasons for their acquisitions. Contributing additional capital to provide for growth is seldom a problem with these buyers because of the financial strength usually associated with strategic buyers. Strategic buyers are more conservative in the financing of an acquisition, putting less burden of debt on a target. The disadvantages of strategic buyers, however, may include a new reporting relationship to a corporate bureaucracy and a limited compensation-package for existing management, which must conform to salary caps of the acquirer.

A financial buyer is more dependent on existing management, and structures a transaction accordingly. Financial buyers are especially sensitive to the entrepreneurial drive that has made a company successful and will change as little as possible after the acquisition. They will often give to current management a minority shared ownership and creative packages for compensation as a motivator, allowing them a share in the future success of the company.

At any given time, there are a number of financial buyers planning consolidations in many industries. Existing management in these industries may help the financial buyers to effect such consolidations. Existing management may help the financial buyer make other acquisitions in the industry to create value in a "roll up." The financial rewards to participating management in building and selling a successful "roll up" can be enormous.

Disadvantages of selling to financial buyers may include a structured transaction with less cash at closing and more consideration, such as sellers' notes and earnouts based on future performance of the company. A financial buyer will usually require a longer transitional period for retaining the seller's management of the purchased company. This may conflict with an owner's desire to retire sooner rather than later. Depending on market conditions, financial buyers also may have greater difficulty in raising financing from a bank to fund acquisitions, if the market is one in which the banking community has an aversion to leveraged buyouts.

An important point to remember when considering the sale of your company is that multiple buyers provide you with choices concerning the best partner. The purchase price paid at the closing is only one consideration. Since selling a business is a complicated process, it is more important than ever to work with a skilled professional who can create a competitive environment to generate multiple selling options for you.

2. Know what your choices are in looking for buyers.

Vendors. Many business owners neglect to consider vendors as potential buyers, but my experience is that they can become excellent buyers, especially when they have developed strategic plans for growth that include vertical integration. In many situations a vendor can accelerate growth by acquiring a customer and then supplying all of the customer's requirements. Such acquisitions contain the potential for higher returns, since the buyer is receiving a return for the profits of the acquired firm and for the sales it is making to the acquired firm.

Competitors. Competitors are logical buyers for any company, but a great deal of care should be exercised, because dealing with competitors is risky. A more detailed discussion on the problems in selling to competitors is contained in Rule 15.

Customers. Customers can also be potential acquirers in situations in which it would make strategic sense to integrate vertically through the acquisition of a supplier. Customers who are manufacturers are normally the most active in acquiring their vendors. Manufacturers typically are searching for acquisitions that would increase their technologic base or strengthen their position to make them a more dominant competitor. Before you contact a customer, determine whether the acquisition of your company would make that customer a more dominant competitor. If so, that customer could be an excellent potential buyer.

One word of caution — offering to discuss the sale of your business with a customer can create a risky situation if the business is not sold. I recommend that you never commence discussions with a customer unless you are working with an experienced mergers-and-acquisitions advisor who has dealt with such situations before. This is a delicate but potentially profitable situation that is best dealt with by calling upon prior experience.

Employees. Selling to employees is a natural inclination of many business owners. Either they feel a sense of loyalty to their employees and want to give them an opportunity to own the business, or they approach employees because it appears to be an easy way to find a buyer. My experience, however, is that employees should only be considered as buyers as a last resort. Dealing with employees first can negatively impact your opportunities to sell the business to an outsider. This topic is extremely important and will be dealt with at length in Rule 15.

Financial buyers. Over the last fifteen years, financial buyers have been among the most active group of buyers for privately owned middle-market companies. The main difference between financial buyers and other buyers is that this group of buyers is purchasing a business as an investment. Typically backed by pension funds, insurance companies, or individuals with high net worth, financial buyers purchase businesses to generate attractive returns that are realized five to seven years later, either by reselling the business or taking it public. Financial buyers always leverage transactions as much as possible. In many transactions, they require the seller to take back notes, non-competes, or other forms of future payments as part of the purchase price. They also frequently allow management of the company, which may include the seller, to have a minority stake in the company and may provide management with generous compensation packages and a share in the future success of the company.

There are probably over 1,000 groups of financial buyers in the United States alone. There are no directories that list all of these groups of financial buyers. Instead, their existence and criteria for acquisitions are contained in well-developed databases maintained by the better professionals in mergers and acquisitions. Make sure that your mergers-and-acquisitions advisor has such a database.

Foreign buyers. Foreign buyers continue to account for a high percentage of all the buyers in reported transactions. Foreign buyers pay the highest prices in all-cash transactions. Their acquisitions usually are strategic and are normally add-ons to existing businesses, either at home or in the U. S. The appetite of foreign buyers is, however, not limited to strategic add-ons. Many foreign buyers desire to broaden their base of U.S. business. To do so, many have developed strategic plans to enter industries that they are not currently in.

The interesting aspect of these plans is that foreign buyers usually pay big premiums for the initial acquisition they make in new industries. For this reason, it is important to expand your dealings with foreign buyers beyond the identified strategic players. Remember, though, that it is difficult, if not impossible, for a business owner to identify and contact large foreign acquirers. If you want to access this important category of buyers, you will not be able to do it alone. Make sure the mergers-and-acquisitions professional you hire has contacts in Europe and the Pacific Rim and has completed transactions in which American client companies were sold to foreign acquirers.

Public and private operating companies. Public and private operating companies usually acquire businesses that are strategically related or are add-ons to their existing businesses. These acquirers look upon acquisitions as an alternative avenue for growth. Typically, these companies are interested in expanding their operations to markets they are not currently in. They see an acquisition as preferable to starting a new division from scratch to serve that particular market. In such cases, the maximum prices paid for acquisitions are normally measured against the cost of successfully starting up an operation from scratch.

Public and private operating companies tend to be cash buyers that pay prices approaching and sometimes exceeding prices paid by foreign buyers. This is because such buyers attach a high value to transactions that fulfill a long-term strategic need. A premium price is not guaranteed, however, so the use of the competitive auctioning process (where the business is sold without an asking price) is still called for in this situation. And in fact, when dealing with this kind of buyer, it is possible to create a competitive bidding process even though there are no other competitors.

This was exactly the situation several years ago when I was representing a highly profitable Midwestern manufacturer of specialized medical products. We had just begun discussions with a large public company that turned out to be the eventual buyer. At that time, the best offer we had received for my client's business was $14 million. The public company's first offer was $18 million. Although my client was delighted with the offer and wanted to accept it, we were selling without an asking price, and I had led the public company to believe that there were other competitors at higher prices even though *actually* there were none. The client agreed to allow me to test the buyer's price elasticity using the auction selling technique.

To determine the maximum strategic value placed by the buyer on my client's company, I responded that the $18 million was not enough, because we had better offers from other buyers. Then we learned how badly this buyer wanted this company. The strategic need had to be exceptional because, through a series of offers and counter-offers, we were able to move the price up to $27 million, and in all that time the buyer was competing against itself, but never knew it. That buyer paid $27 million when it could have purchased the company for $18 million.

This example illustrates the difference in price that can be generated by a professional skilled in the technique of selling without an asking price combined with the competitive auctioning process. In my more than 20 years of experience in closing more than 75 deals, a common thread that seems to run through each transaction is that the skills I employ in manipulating buyers always produce premium selling prices for my clients. For this reason, I always tell my clients, "You do not pay me a fee; I earn it."

Strategic buyers have the greatest potential for paying the highest prices, and only experienced mergers-and-acquisitions professionals are capable of extracting these prices.

If you want to sell for the highest price, make sure that you are represented by the *best mergers-and-acquisitions* professional you can find.

Don't be concerned if the best professional charges more. The return on investment will be immediate and obvious.

> **TYPES OF POTENTIAL BUYERS**
> - **Vendors**
> - **Competitors**
> - **Customers**
> - **Employees**
> - **Financial buyers/investment groups**
> - **Foreign buyers**
> - **Public and private operating companies**

3. Know how to locate potential buyers.

If you decide to ignore a significant piece of advice in this book and proceed with a plan to sell your business yourself, it is likely that the first limitation confronting you will be in finding resources with which to locate buyers. Therefore, it is best to take a common sense approach in developing your list of potential buyers. The first step should be to identify those companies or groups of financial buyers who would be the most logical buyers for the business. This includes competitors, vendors, customers, or known investment groups whose businesses would be enhanced by a merger with your company. You can expand the list beyond companies you already know, through research on public and private companies in the business reference section at a large public library or on the internet. Add to this list the names of buyers who have approached you in the past when you weren't interested in selling. Keep in mind that these buyers may no longer be interested, but in any event they could be good sources of leads for other potential buyers.

Depending upon the situation, advertising in publications such as local newspapers and business journals and in your industry trade papers or in *The Wall Street Journal* can be an effective way to develop interested buyers. Advertising, however, is usually used only in the sale of smaller companies, so it may not be appropriate for your situation. Remember, when you advertise, it is very likely that you will breach any wall of confidentiality you have set up to prevent your customers, competitors, and employees from learning about your desire to sell. Notwithstanding its potential to develop leads on buyers, advertising should only be used as a last resort and preferably with the advice of an experienced professional.

It is best to use a mergers-and-acquisitions professional to locate buyers.

Locating buyers is one of the most important skills that a mergers-and-acquisitions professional brings to the transaction. Remember, when you select a professional you will look for someone who has the contacts and resources needed to identify the large number of potential buyers required to sell your business for the highest price. Many M&A professionals maintain extensive databases of buyers that can instantly provide the names of hundreds of qualified buyers. They also can call upon other people in their organizations and on the wealth of experience they have gained in dealing with buyers in other transactions.

Even better, many mergers-and-acquisitions professionals will have experience in handling transactions in your particular industry, and they will know the strategic plans of most of the acquirers. Many also have ongoing contacts with a number of overseas buyers, their investment bankers, and financial advisors. Such contacts are absolutely critical to developing interest from foreign buyers. Finally, top-notch mergers-and-acquisitions professionals are constantly dealing with all of the key financial acquirers. They are aware of their criteria for acquisitions and the potential for investment in your business.

Locating a number of qualified buyers to run an auction requires the skill and knowledge that is only possessed by a mergers-and-acquisitions professional.

RULE 13

Obtain the highest possible selling price for your business by selling to a premium buyer.

To sell your business for the highest possible price, you must involve premium buyers in the sale process. Premium buyers have a number of common attributes. Typically, they are large organizations (public or private) with substantial financial resources, which are interested in acquisitions that fit within criteria established for their strategic plan for growth. The need to find acquisitions with a strategic fit creates the ability to pay the highest prices for those acquisitions. Generally, premium buyers fall into one of the four specific categories described below. If you are dealing with a buyer included in one of these categories, you can assume you are dealing with a buyer capable of paying the highest price.

1. Foreign companies, public and private.

Foreign companies pay the highest prices for acquisitions of all the categories of premium buyers. There are several reasons behind their pricing expectations. First, foreign companies are inclined to add a premium to the cost of acquiring a U.S. company. Such a premium is perceived as the acquirer's cost of entering the lucrative U.S. market. Fluctuations in currency also have a direct bearing on the price that foreign buyers can pay. When conditions cause a decline in the value of the U.S. dollar compared to the national currency of the acquirer, the acquisition of U.S. companies can be effected relatively cheaply when compared to making the same kind of acquisitions in the home country. On the other hand, if the dollar rises in value, acquisitions become more expensive and less attractive to foreign buyers.

2. Public companies in the U.S.

Domestic public companies are premium buyers because generally they only make acquisitions that synergistically and strategically fit into their long-term plans for growth. They can pay high prices because they have the ability to make 2 + 2 equal 6. Or, to put it another way, by combining acquired businesses with existing businesses, they can increase profits through growth in sales and savings in costs that are solely attributable to the new business combination. These kinds of buyers are the only ones capable of achieving these values. Therefore, they can justify a higher price.

Domestic public companies have another added advantage in the acquisition arena in that they can offer higher prices to sellers who are willing to swap the stock in their company for stock in the acquiring public company. In a stock swap, the buyer's main concern is dilution. In many instances, the higher offer results because the buyer can offer the seller their stock at a value comparable to or slightly less than its public stock multiple. In addition to a higher sales price, the stock swap offers the seller the opportunity to defer tax on the gain until the newly acquired stock is sold. The negative aspect of the stock swap is the continued market risk that the seller runs while holding the buyer's stock. Also, there could be unattractive restrictions on the sale of the stock that could impede the ability to achieve liquidity freely. On the other hand, if the stock is in companies of good quality, the seller could double or triple the value of the shares by holding them as a long-term investment and maximizing value and tax benefits when the stock is sold.

Another favorable aspect of dealing with domestic public companies is that they do not require special financing to fund acquisitions made for cash. This kind of acquirer has established lines of credit or has cash available to fund acquisitions. This is a critical positive attribute for this type of buyer and a virtue that cannot be overstated. Remember that most of the deals that fall through do so because the buyer cannot obtain financing. If the necessity for finding financing is eliminated, the probabilities increase that the deal will be consummated.

3. Large private companies in the U.S.

Large private companies are generally identical to public companies in the way they view acquisitions. In other words, they want acquisitions that synergistically and strategically fit into their plans for growth. And like their public cousins, large private companies are known for paying high prices for their acquisitions, because their goal in making an acquisition is to combine acquired businesses with existing businesses, thereby increasing profits through savings in costs and growth in sales.

In most cases, large private companies mirror public companies in the process used for acquisitions, but there are two key areas in which these acquirers differ. First, one of the distinct advantages a public company has in making acquisitions is that it can increase the price paid by offering the seller an opportunity to engage in a tax-free exchange for stock in the public company. Another advantage that public companies have is that they are well known or have the ability to provide a seller with 10Ks, 10Qs, annual reports, and other materials which enable the seller to become extremely knowledgeable in the affairs of a public suitor. Private companies, on the other hand, typically do not provide such information. Thus, they are at a disadvantage if they have to compete against a public company. Large private companies do have established lines of credit available, which they can use to fund acquisitions. These buyers not only pay high prices, but they have the ability to fund cash purchases with no need to make separate arrangements for financing.

Lack of financing is the primary reason that acquisitions fail. Your chances of a successful sale are magnified when you deal with foreign, public, or large private companies that do not require special financing to complete acquisitions.

4. Financial buyers making their first acquisition or "platform acquisition" in a specific industry, or making add-on acquisitions to complement the growth of a portfolio company.

Normally, financial buyers would not be considered in the category of premium buyers because they usually purchase businesses as investments. Accordingly, their main criteria for determining the value they place on a potential acquisition is "return on investment." Financial buyers do, however, typically pay substantial premiums to acquire companies that will become a "platform" for further consolidation in a given industry. In calculating return on investment, the group creates a model that represents the projected five-year future income-stream of the business. These earnings are then discounted to a present value and then added to the projected terminal value of the assets of the business after five years. A calculation of the combined result is the maximum value that the group of financial buyers would place on the business.

One important thing to note is that the "return on investment" approach in valuing acquisitions limits the amount that an acquirer can pay to the present value of the future earnings of the business on a stand-alone basis. On the other hand, foreign companies, public companies, and large private companies can pay more than the mere stand-alone value, because they acquire companies that are synergistic to and strategically fit with other businesses that they own. Thus, when such buyers combine an acquired business with businesses that they own, they are able to cause the income of the combined entities to increase to levels that could not be achieved if the entities had not been combined under a single ownership.

There are two situations in which financial buyers approach acquisitions with the same expectations for value as do foreign companies, public companies, and large private companies. These situations arise when (1) the financial buyer is seeking add-on investments to a company in their portfolio or (2) when the financial buyer is preparing to make its first acquisition or a "platform" acquisition in a specific industry. Once you discover that a financial buyer has targeted your company as a potential platform acquisition, you can expect to extract a substantial premium from them. The key is to be aware that you have been targeted as a potential "platform." The transaction I completed in 1996 for Midwestern Distributing Company is an excellent example of how to extract the highest price from a financial buyer once you have determined that you are a targeted platform.

Midwestern Distributors was an Ohio-based specialized food distributing company that distributed only to chains of fast food restaurants. Its equipment, warehouses, and employees were all dedicated to serving the specialized needs of this fast-growing customer-base. The company did approximately $200 million in sales and was growing at about 20 percent per year. The food distributing industry in general had undergone substantial consolidation through 1996, but there had been no effort to consolidate the number of specialized distributors exclusively serving the fast food restaurant industry.

When I took Midwestern into the market, there was a significant level of interest because of the quality of the company and its future prospects for growth. One of the buyers very interested in the deal was the Colorado Equity Fund, a group from Denver doing leveraged buyouts. In assessing the intentions of Colorado Equity, I learned that they had talked to other specialized food distributors serving the fast food industry, regarding a consolidation play. The group had, however, been unable to make its first "platform" acquisition, which was needed to enable them to bring other companies into the fold. Their strategy, I learned, was to acquire companies for cash and stock in the newly consolidated entity. The carrot they would offer sellers was to cash out and still be able to share in the buildup in value of the new, larger entity as the consolidation play unfolded. They badly needed the first acquisition, and they believed Midwestern was the perfect candidate to become the platform for this process.

I received a number of offers for this deal. The better offers, which included the offer from Colorado, were in the range of 7 to 7.5 times EBIT. In the market conditions that existed in 1996, they were considered very good offers and probably reflected the true market value of this business, but I knew that Colorado could pay a lot more because they needed this deal to implement their strategy for consolidation in this industry. Therefore — and this is key — with the knowledge of their need in mind, I proceeded to squeeze Colorado in negotiations to extract the largest premium over real value that they would pay. Ultimately, the result was a deal at ten times EBIT, or $45 million over the maximum value that any of the numerous other buyers saw in this business.

Never forget this example. Always be aware of the possibility that the financial buyer pursuing you is doing so because your company is a potential candidate as a "platform." Ask if they own other businesses similar to yours. Ask if they have strategically identified the industry you are in as being one ripe for consolidation, and if you would be their first of a number of acquisitions they plan to make to achieve consolidation. You must determine the buyer's strategic goal in wanting to acquire your company. Once you determine that, you will know whether they would be prepared to pay a significant premium to acquire your company.

Always find the reason for the financial buyer's interest in your business.

TYPES OF PREMIUM BUYERS
- **Foreign companies, public and private**
- **Public companies in the U.S.**
- **Large private companies in the U.S.**
- **Financial buyers making their first acquisition
   or "platform" acquisition in a specific industry,
   or making add-on acquisitions to a company
   in their portfolio**

RULE 14

Understand the buyer's mentality.

Educate yourself on how buyers view transactions and on what motivates them. Be aware of the choices confronting every buyer who expresses an interest in acquiring your firm. What puts the buyer in the driver's seat is having the choice of either acquiring your company or someone else's company. If you have a business that is exceptional and unique, the buyer may not be able to find an acceptable alternative candidate. In that event, leverage shifts from the buyer to the seller. On the other hand, if you know that there are other businesses like yours that could be acquired, you had better do a superb job of convincing the buyer that, of all the businesses available, yours is the best.

1. The only way to create a sense of urgency with buyers is to sell through the competitive auctioning process.
When you deal with buyers, keep this in mind: *You may have to sell your business for various personal or economic reasons, but seldom will you come in contact with a buyer who has to buy.* Rarely will their mindset see the same sense of urgency that you have.

2. All strategic acquirers have the option of acquiring your business, acquiring another one like it, or starting up such a business from scratch.
A typical approach for strategic buyers in determining the maximum value they will pay for your business is to compare that price to the cost of build-

ing a startup operation and making it profitable. Remember, strategic buyers always have the option of starting a business from scratch, and that places a cap on the value that they will pay for your business. A seller who understands the total economics of a startup alternative scenario would be at an advantage in negotiating with this type of buyer.

3. The more you know about the buyers' needs, the more leverage you will have when you negotiate with them.

Knowing the buyers' needs is a critical element in understanding what motivates them. Are these buyers acquiring for investment only? Are they looking for a specific fit with one of their existing businesses? The buyer looking for the specific fit has a higher level of need than the plain vanilla investor does. Determine if this buyer is a financial buyer that has raised money but has not yet completed their first investment. If so, there could be a great deal of pressure on that buyer to get this first deal completed. Such knowledge could be of enormous help to you as the seller when you negotiate with that buyer.

Here are some other questions to which the answers will give insights into the buyers' mentality:

How do they price the businesses they acquire? Do they purchase on the basis of values computed using the present value of discounted cash flow, multiples of net worth, multiples of earnings before interest and taxes, or using other computational techniques for assessing value? If you know how they determine value, you will know the maximum prices they will pay.

If the buyer has purchased companies before, what have they done with prior acquisitions? Are they long-term players buying for investment, or do they purchase and resell after three to five years? Find out how they have treated the management and employees of the companies they acquire. If your research discloses that their main interest lies in acquiring good management, then structure your presentation to focus on the strengths of your managerial team.

The reason to be "educated" in regard to buyers is to be able to focus on their needs. If you can convince them that your business satisfies their needs, they will most likely offer a high price to buy it.

RULE 15

Do not sell to employees or competitors.

There is an important reason why I have included this rule. My experience in dealing with this category of buyers has proven that they can create any number of significant problems that can either negatively impact your ability to sell the business or can adversely impact the future performance of the business regardless of whether it is sold.

1. Never consider selling to employees unless other acceptable buyers cannot be found.

Employees usually do not have the funds to supply the equity needed to conclude the deal. If you get involved in a sales transaction to your employees, you may find yourself financing most of their investment. You may have to take back employees' notes and use other structures to supplement the pool of equity available within the group of employees. If the employees have limited funds going into the deal, what happens if there is a problem and the business requires additional capital? The answer is: The employee-owners will have to find new investors to back them and, if they can't, the business and your notes and future payments would be in jeopardy. Since most sales to employees require additional borrowing, the transaction creates pressures on the business because of the obligations created to pay interest and principal. Another negative result of this maximum leverage is that it creates financial constraints on the future growth of the business. The heavy debt-load will adversely affect the ability of the business to take advantage of new opportunities to expand and grow.

Employees seldom pay the highest price. This is mainly because employees who become buyers cannot realistically be part of a competitive auctioning process. Outside buyers believe that a harmonious relationship with the management and employees of a newly acquired company is essential for future success. It is this driving desire for a good working relationship with management that makes most buyers reluctant to compete with management in a bidding war for the business. Thus, most buyers will exit from the bidding process as soon as they learn they are bidding against management. This is one of the principal reasons that I advise clients to avoid including employees as potential buyers.

Attempted sales to employees drive away other buyers. Most other potential buyers will be skeptical of purchasing your business after they discover that you first tried to sell to your employees and failed. Buyers view such businesses as "damaged goods," tainted by the failed buyout by the employees. The buyer's perception is that the failed buyout created ill will that will carry over to the new owners. The astute buyer will say: "Who needs this kind of problem? Let's find another deal."

If you insist on pursuing a sale to your employees, it will likely result in the elimination of many of the best-qualified buyers. Take my advice. Sell to employees only as a last resort.

2. Avoid including competitors as potential buyers for your business.

Many entrepreneurs believe that a competitor will be the logical buyer for their business. When they decide to sell, they will contact competitors directly to promote a deal. Or, in some cases, a competitor will initiate the contact with the seller and offer to buy the business. But if you have a good business, you don't have to sell it to a competitor. There are a vast number of qualified buyers ready to pay very high prices for such a business. Bear in mind that dealing with competitors is extremely risky and can backfire if the business is not sold. Generally speaking, dealing with competitors does not result in satisfactory transactions for the seller for a number of reasons.

Your confidentiality will be breached. Confidentiality should be of paramount concern when you sell your business. Dealing with competitors creates a higher risk of breaking the confidentiality surrounding the sale. A competitor has no reason to assist you in maintaining confidentiality with your customers and employees.

It is also difficult to know if competitors are sincere purchasers or merely "tire kickers," anxious to learn as much as possible about how you do business. Through the normal investigative process involved in purchasing a company, competitors will find out many "company secrets" that are better kept out of the hands of competitors. Unfortunately, this is a risk of the selling process. You cannot sell your company unless you disclose to potential buyers how the business operates and, particularly, why it is successful vis-a-vis the competition. In all transactions, potential buyers sign confidentiality agreements and agree not to disclose or use the information provided to the buyer by the seller. As a practical matter, however, a competitor will make use of such knowledge and could damage the future sales and profits of the selling company.

Even when the competitor is a sincere purchaser, damage can be done to the future of your business if the deal doesn't go through.

Disclosing sensitive information to competitors can also negatively impact the interest of non-competing potential buyers. They may back away from a transaction when they discover that a major competitor has been involved in pursuing the acquisition and has become privy to most of the secrets of the business. They believe, and rightly so, that the future profitability of the business may have been adversely affected by such disclosure.

Competitors normally do not pay the highest price. Competitors will have a greater sense of the value of your business and understand its potential better than outsiders. They tend to discount the potential more than an outsider would, since they have the option of expansion of their own business or growth by acquisition. In addition, competitors may simply take the position that they will try to steal the business for a low price. If they can't buy it for that, they will still benefit from having pursued the transaction because of all the inside knowledge they obtain about the business. I refer to these buyers as "bargain basement tire kickers." Dealing with them offers nothing to the prospective seller except added risk and exposure.

Your loyal employees might be hurt. Most of my clients have an organization of loyal, dedicated employees, many of whom have assisted in building the business over a number of years. Most sellers have a sense of loyalty to their employees and desire to see the business in the hands of a new owner that will grow the business and protect their jobs. Competitors, however, normally maximize profits from acquisitions by effecting consolidations, staff reductions, and selling off of assets from the acquired business. A sale to a competitor is likely to result in the business, as you know it, disappearing and many of your loyal employees being terminated.

Avoid dealing with competitors or approach them only as a last resort when no other acceptable buyers have been located.

RULE 16

Keep the sale process confidential.

In every deal, without exception, the major concern expressed by entrepreneurs is that their competitors, customers, employees, and others will discover that their business is for sale. Many entrepreneurs I talk to tell me they want to sell their business, but they are reluctant to proceed out of fear that their desire to sell will become known and have an undesirable impact on the business. If you have concerns about problems with confidentiality in the selling process, rest assured that your concerns are a universal reflection of the community of business owners. Notwithstanding those concerns, I have been involved in over 75 transactions in which I sold privately held businesses, and in every case, I was able to keep the process confidential until the sale was consummated. There are a number of tried and true rules I have employed over the years to protect the confidentiality of the selling process.

The best way to maintain confidentiality during the selling process is to retain a professional mergers-and-acquisitions intermediary who understands the need for confidentiality and has the experience and knowledge needed to maintain confidentiality throughout the selling process.

1. My "common sense" rules to protect the confidentiality of the transaction:

Avoid dealing with competitors as potential buyers. Competitors have a tendency to "leak" information about the sale to the industry. Remember that such leaks can hurt your business but at the same time can benefit your competitors.

Avoid dealing with customers as potential buyers. Customers will not leak information intentionally, because they have nothing to gain from the dissemination of such knowledge. If your customers are also dealing with your competitors, however, information may "accidentally" leak to one of those competitors. Once such information is in the hands of a competitor, it tends to spread quickly throughout the industry.

Don't negotiate to sell the business to employees. Once your employees learn of your intentions, the information will quickly spread to your competitors and customers.

Restrict the involvement of employees in the selling process. Usually I advise clients to limit the involvement of employees with buyers to include only the owners, key individuals in management (only if they will greatly increase the value of the business), and the company's chief financial officer if he or she is needed to provide financial information for the sale. I never involve any other employees or inform them about the prospective sale.

Avert rumors about "visitors" to your business. When a business is being sold, "strangers" — potential buyers and their advisors — will be visiting the company headquarters and its operating facilities regularly. Strangers in facilities create rumors and speculation among employees about who they are and why they are there. To preempt such rumors, develop a "reason" for these visits and inform your employees about it. "Reasons" used by my clients have included seeking new banking relationships, raising capital for growth, and looking for a new facility to expand. If you preempt the rumor mill, you can channel employees' thoughts into other areas and protect the confidentiality of the selling process.

I always place a limit on visits to clients' facilities by potential buyers until a deal has been agreed to and due diligence has begun. It is a good idea to find an alternative site to hold meetings with prospective buyers, such as hotels, restaurants, and private clubs. If you can keep prospective buyers out of your facility, you can reduce the risk of damaging rumors being started by your employees.

Screen prospective buyers thoroughly before they are given information on the company. There may be conflicts with potential buyers that you are unaware of unless you do your homework. I have found instances where some of the buyer's employees or directors had relationships with competitors or customers that could result in a leak of confidential information. For this reason, it is important to screen potential buyers thoroughly to make sure that such conflicts are not present in their organizations.

2. Always have potential buyers sign a confidentiality agreement before you provide them with any information on the company.

Mergers-and-acquisitions professionals have their own confidentiality agreements, which are used in all of their transactions. If you are not using a mergers-and-acquisitions professional, have your attorney prepare a confidentiality agreement that you can use in the sale process. The text of the confidentiality agreement that I use follows. ⌒

Confidentiality Agreement

As you requested in connection with your possible interest in purchasing _____ (the "Company"), we are furnishing to you, upon your execution and delivery to us of this letter of agreement, certain information about the operations of the Company. All information about the Company furnished by us or our affiliates, or our respective directors, officers, employees, agents or controlling persons (such affiliates and other persons collectively referred to herein as "Representatives"), is referred to in this letter of agreement as "Proprietary Information." Proprietary Information does not include, however, information which (a) is or becomes generally available to the public other than as a result of a disclosure by you or your Representatives, (b) was available to you on a nonconfidential basis prior to its disclosure by us or (c) becomes available to you on a nonconfidential basis from a person other than us who is not otherwise bound by a confidentiality agreement with us or our Representatives. As used in this letter, the term "person" shall be broadly interpreted to include, without limitation, any corporation, company, partnership and individual.

Unless otherwise agreed to in writing by us, you agree (a) except as required by law, to keep all Proprietary Information confidential and not to disclose or reveal any Proprietary Information to any person other than those employed by you or on your behalf who are actively and directly participating in the evaluation of a possible acquisition of the Company (the "Proposed Transaction") or who otherwise need to know the Proprietary Information for the purpose of evaluating the Proposed Transaction and to cause those persons to observe the terms of this letter of agreement and (b) not to use Proprietary Information for any purpose other than in connection with the consummation of the Proposed Transaction in a manner which we have approved. You will be responsible for any breach of the terms hereunder by you or the persons or entities referred to in subparagraph (a) of this paragraph. In the event that you are requested pursuant to, or required by, applicable law or regulation or by legal process to disclose any Proprietary Information, you agree that you will provide us with prompt notice of such request(s) to enable us to seek an appropriate protective order.

Unless otherwise required by law, neither you nor your Representatives will, without our prior written consent, disclose to any person (other than those actively and directly participating in the Proposed Transaction) any information about the Proposed Transaction, or the terms, conditions or other facts relating thereto, including the fact that discussions are taking place with respect thereto or the status thereof, or the fact that the Proprietary Information has been made available to you.

Confidentiality Agreement - page 2

In no case will you disclose to any person (other than those actively and directly participating in the Proposed Transaction) that the owner of the Company is considering a possible sale. In no case will you contact any employee of the Company without our permission.

If you determine that you do not wish to proceed with the Proposed Transaction, you will promptly advise us of that decision. In that case, or in the event that the Proposed Transaction is not consummated by you, you will promptly deliver to us all of the Proprietary Information, including all copies, reproductions, summaries, analyses or extracts thereof or based thereon in your possession or in the possession of any of your Representatives. You further agree that for a period of two years from the date hereof you will not solicit the employment of any of the employees of the Company while they are employees of the Company.

Although the Proprietary Information contains information which we believe to be relevant for the purpose of your evaluation of the Proposed Transaction, we do not make any representation or warranty as to the accuracy or completeness of the Proprietary Information. Neither we, our affiliates, nor any of our respective officers, directors, employees, agents or controlling persons shall have any liability to you or any of your Representatives relating to or arising from the use of the Proprietary Information.

This Agreement shall inure to the benefit of Company and shall be enforceable by it without limitation.

Please confirm your agreement with the foregoing by signing and returning to the undersigned the duplicate copy of this letter enclosed herewith.

Goldfarb Financial
Chicago, IL

By: _____
Steven G. Goldfarb
Managing Director

Accepted and Agreed to this
____day of_____, 2001

By: _____

Title: _____

PART III

What You Need TO KNOW

About the Sale Process

SECTION 1

Issues That Could Cause Your Sale To Fail

Once you begin the process, you'll want to complete the sale of your business as quickly as possible. A seller's worst nightmare is to spend months going through the sale process, finding a buyer, and negotiating a good deal — only to have the deal fall apart before the expected closing. There are a number of things that can cause a deal to go wrong, and in most cases they can be avoided if the seller is educated and prepared to deal with these problems.

1. A sale can fail when the seller is represented by the wrong attorney.

This is the number one problem that causes deals to fall apart. As a former practicing attorney, I can speak about this issue with a great deal of authority. When most entrepreneurs start their businesses, they form a relationship with an attorney who is either a solo practitioner or part of a small firm. More often than not, the entrepreneur continues that relationship. Some business owners recognize the limits of such attorneys and, as their business grows, they seek out counsel at larger, more sophisticated law firms. Because of the additional cost, however, most entrepreneurs elect to stay with "old tried and true."

"Old tried and true" may be a good lawyer — probably a general practitioner who handles everything from divorce to real estate to litigation. But it is highly unlikely that he or she specializes in mergers and acquisitions or has much experience in the complexities of the ever-changing laws in the field. Your attorney is probably not an expert in securities law and probably has never advised on a transaction like the one you are contemplating, or if he has, it has been on an infrequent basis. But notwithstanding the lack of knowledge or experience, "old tried and true" will likely see your transaction as a nice piece of business, making it unlikely that you will get the advice you need: *Use a specialist.*

I have always found this point intriguing. We live in an age of specialization. When you have a tax problem, you use a tax lawyer, for labor problems you use a labor lawyer, and for an environmental problem, an environmental lawyer. But, for a mergers-and-acquisitions problem, owners continue to turn to "old tried and true." Why? Why not a mergers-and-acquisitions lawyer? Doesn't that make sense? It should, because with the right lawyer, you will greatly increase the odds that your deal will close.

The best investment you can make is to hire a top-notch mergers-and-acquisitions attorney. It costs more, but in the long run, it'll be much cheaper because your deal will be done.

2. A sale can fail when the seller refuses to accept continuing liability.

Many sellers believe that selling a business is a relatively simple process. They expect the closing to be simply an exchange in which they turn over their stock or title to the business assets to the buyer and, in return, they receive cash and just walk away. It may have been this simple years ago, but that is no longer the case. Today, we live in a litigious society, and you can no longer just walk away. Today a seller is expected to provide the buyer with a number of representations and warranties that survive the closing of the sale. *Representations and warranties* are statements made by the seller about the condition of the business, its assets, liabilities, contracts, financial statements, and many other areas that the buyer relied upon in making the decision to purchase. These representations and warranties create potential liability for the seller. It is essential that you understand these risks before you enter into an agreement.

A seller must understand that the *only way* to sell a business today is by agreeing to provide the buyer with customary representations and warranties. I have seen transactions terminated at the last minute when the seller refuses to accept this continuing liability and backs out of the deal. A deal should never be terminated for that reason. This is another reason you need a knowledgeable mergers-and-acquisitions attorney. Your attorney will counsel you about representations and warranties long before the closing of the sale. As an educated seller, you will enter into the process expecting to provide the buyer with traditional representations and warranties. In addition, a mergers-and-acquisitions attorney with experience in negotiating numerous similar agreements will be in the best position to minimize your exposure.

3. A sale can fail when the seller does not make full disclosure during the sale process.

In every sale you, the seller, will make a number of representations about the business, which the buyer will rely on in making a decision to purchase. After you and the buyer reach an agreement in principle on the sale (a letter of intent), the buyer will commence due diligence for the purpose of verifying that all the representations made are true. As a seller, you should never underestimate the ability of the buyer to discover hidden problems during due diligence. If problems are there, they will probably be found, and in many cases, that discovery can lead to the termination of the deal. *Always make complete and total disclosure to the buyer.* By taking this approach, you protect yourself from potential litigation and prevent "surprises" that might come out of the buyer's process of due diligence.

I recognize that you may have problems in your business that you would be concerned about disclosing because of the potentially adverse impact on the buyer. I assure you, however, *the buyer will eventually find out about these problems.* The best advice I can give is to disclose the problem early in the process. You can always frame the problem in the best possible light to minimize the impact on the buyer. This approach works. By controlling the disclosure, you can minimize the impact and prevent the deal from cratering later on.

4. A sale can fail when the seller cannot satisfy concerns about environmental laws and regulations.

Every year, more and more transactions are being terminated because of the seller's inability to satisfy the buyer's concerns about environmental problems related to the business. Buyers' environmental concerns are the greatest in transactions where the buyer is purchasing the real estate used by the business. As a general rule, buyers will not purchase businesses where the real estate contains environmental problems.

How do you avoid having environmental problems kill your deal? Before you put the company up for sale, retain a qualified environmental engineering firm to make a "phase one inspection" of your property. If problems are discovered, clean them up before you take the company to market. Remember: These problems will be discovered by the buyer during the process of due diligence. When the buyer discovers the problems, one of two things will happen. Either you will be required to clean up the problems, or the deal will be terminated. So, why take the risk? Clean up the problems before you take the company to market.

5. A sale can fail when the buyer discovers a change in the condition of the business (sales and profits) during the final phases of the transaction.

Buyers closely watch the performance of the business during this period. If sales and profits start to decline, they will immediately become concerned about potential negative trends and may elect to terminate their interest in the deal. For this reason, *you should do everything you can to maintain continued positive trends in sales and profits during the final phases of the transaction.* This is the time to redouble your diligence in the management of the firm.

Just because you have reached an agreement in principle doesn't mean that the deal will close. Don't let anything slip between the cracks. That mistake or misjudgment can easily kill your deal.

6. A sale can fail when the seller has problems with transfer of contracted rights.

If the existence of your business is dependent on certain contracted rights (e.g., licenses, franchises, distribution rights), make sure you have the ability to transfer these rights to the new owner. You must ascertain the transferability of such rights and any problems that could prevent a transfer, before you put your company up for sale. I have seen a number of transactions where the seller discovered late in the sale process that certain of these rights could not be transferred. The result of that disclosure was that the buyer terminated the deal.

Remember that these rights are essential to the continued success of the business. Without these rights, there is no business to sell. For example, if you own a Coca-Cola distributorship, before you market the business, determine the required procedure for transferring the distributorship. Then find out what is required of you and the buyer in order to effect the buyer's ownership. If you discover potential problems, find the solutions in advance. By being educated on the requirements for a transfer you can prevent this from being an issue that kills your deal.

7. A sale can fail when the buyer has problems with its financing.

A failure by the buyer to obtain financing for the deal is a major reason for sales being terminated. Any transaction containing a condition for financing from the buyer is potentially in trouble. Inability to finance the deal could be caused by events that are beyond the buyer's control, such as changes in the credit markets. In almost every case where financing is not achieved, however, the buyer's failure can be attributed to two principal factors. The first and most important factor is that the buyer has not put enough equity into the deal. In the past, buyers could go forward with transactions with almost nothing down. Today, a buyer must be prepared to put a significant amount of equity into the deal. Knowing this should put you on notice to determine how much equity the buyer plans to put into the deal before you sign a letter of intent. If the amount appears to be insufficient to get the deal done, you will be well served to demand that the buyer increase the commitment of equity before you sign a letter of intent.

The second principal factor is the failure to secure financing for the mezzanine portion of the acquisition debt. Most privately held businesses are Sub-Chapter S corporations. Their net worth is typically substantively less than the sale price for the business. In transactions like these, traditional senior lenders will lend only on the basis of their loans being secured by the assets of the business. But the combination of senior debt and equity may not be sufficient to finance the deal. If additional financing is required, the buyer must seek out mezzanine or subordinated lenders to fill the gap. These lenders normally lend on the basis of cash flow, and their loans are really a form of de facto equity. The biggest problem with financing transactions in the middle market today is that it is extremely difficult to find sources of mezzanine financing for most deals. Should your deal require your buyer to obtain mezzanine financing, you had better determine in advance of signing the letter of intent that the buyer has a source of such financing and can obtain it to close the deal.

If the buyer can't deliver on the mezzanine financing, the alternative left to you is to assume that portion of the financing with seller's notes, or to terminate the deal. Neither of these alternatives is particularly attractive. If you retain nothing else from this book, remember this: The more you know about the buyer's financing capabilities, the more likely it is that you will be dealing with a buyer who can get the deal done. The worst thing you can do is waste months dealing with a buyer who cannot finance your deal.

After you have explored a buyer's financing capabilities, if you have any doubts about their ability to finance the deal, consider dealing with another buyer.

ISSUES THAT COULD CAUSE YOUR SALE TO FAIL
1. **Representation by the wrong attorney**
2. **Refusing to accept continuing liability**
3. **Lack of full disclosure**
4. **Unsatisfied concerns about environmental regulations**
5. **Change in sales/profits during the final phases of selling**
6. **Problems with transfer of contracted rights**
7. **Buyer's problems with financing**

SECTION 2

How To Sell Without an Asking Price

If your priority is to sell your business for the highest possible price, then this is the most important chapter in the book. "Most important chapter in the book?" you say. "Why is it so important to sell without an asking price?" Because an asking price effectively places a cap on the amount of money you can sell your business for. Then you may say, "Well, I just sold my home for a huge price, more than anyone thought it was worth. I knew the market was hot, so I listed it for more than I thought it was worth. And guess what? It sold for that price in three days."

But wouldn't you also have to say, "If I sold my home in three days at that price, maybe I should have asked for more!" The asking price you listed limited the amount you could obtain, and you will never know if the value could have been higher. *The only way to know is to sell without an asking price.* Now, understand this: I am not advocating that real estate transactions be done without asking prices. Having an asking price on all real estate listings is customary and expected by all buyers. If you want to sell real estate, you have to disclose an asking price.

However, we are discussing the sale of a business — not real estate — and the rules of that game are a lot more flexible. Let us be clear on this very important point: In sales of businesses, there is no custom or expectation among buyers that every business for sale has an asking price. That doesn't mean that buyers won't ask you for your asking price, however. It is in their best interest to have one. But, there are ways to get them to make offers without an asking price, and that's why this chapter is so important.

1. Why a business can be sold without an asking price.

Entirely different factors are employed to value businesses than are used to value real estate. Therefore, a different sales approach can be used to sell a business. Real estate can be valued objectively on the basis of a number of factors such as values for land, comparable sales, cost to build per square foot, capitalized value of rents, quality of tenants, length of leases, and so on. Business values are a lot more subjective, based on what individual buyers believe the business is worth. This will vary significantly from buyer to buyer.

An excellent example of this is a large chain of beauty salons that I sold in the early 1990s.

The company had 35 salons in major malls around the U.S. Sales were $24.5 million and the company generated approximately $3 million a year in cash flow. The ultimate buyer was also in the salon business and operated approximately the same number of salons in a region of the U.S. that complemented the business of the chain that was being sold. My client had about $1.5 million in overhead expenses. The buyer calculated that its administrative organization could take over most of the overhead functions that my client was paying for and could save $1 million per year through a consolidation of the overhead functions.

In addition, even though my client's salons operated in major regional malls, they did a poor job in selling hair products at retail. At the time of sale, my client's sales of retail products were only 10 percent of total revenue. On the other hand, the buyer had a fabulous retail program in its salons, netting 30 percent of revenue. The buyer believed that by installing its program, retail sales could quickly triple in the acquired salons, translating to $4.9 million in new retail sales at a 50 percent markup, or $2.45 million of additional cash flow per year. Taking into account the perceived benefits from the acquired company, the buyer was looking at the following as its cash flow after acquisition:

Projected Cash Flow After Acquisition of the Chain of Salons	
Cash flow currently generated by seller's salons	$ 3,000,000
Reduction in overhead from consolidation of administrative functions	$ 1,000,000
Additional cash flow from increased retail sales of products	$ 2,450,000
Anticipated first-year profit under new ownership	$ 6,450,000

The buyer ultimately paid $22 million for this chain of salons, which was $8 million more than the next highest bidder. The buyer's analysis indicated that the business was worth more to them, and they could afford to pay a premium to buy it. The other buyers were basing their offers on the $3 million in cash flow of the business as operated by the seller.

It's obvious that the $22 million selling price would never have been realized if an asking price had been placed on the business.

The salon transaction is typical of most of the deals I have completed in the past 20 years. In almost every one of these deals, one buyer steps up and offers to pay a price that is substantially greater than that offered by all of the others. Why does that happen? It is because of the synergies and the subjectivity involved in the process of valuation. Only the buyers know what it is worth to them. Only a process of selling without an asking price can get that value onto the table. Buyers will place high valuations on the table because:

◆ They don't know who the other bidders are or what they are willing to pay.

◆ They have concluded that the business is worth that much to them, and they are willing to pay it if they have to.

◆ They offer as much as they can, because they want to make sure they are the ultimate buyer.

An excellent example of such a transaction was the sale of a Midwest-based manufacturer of industrial controls that I handled in 1997. The company had sales of $12 million and operating profit of $2 million a year. The historical and projected rate of growth for the business was 20 percent. I received these eight offers to purchase the company:

◆ two offers of $10 million

◆ one offer of $11 million

◆ three offers of $12 million

◆ one offer of $12.5 million

◆ one offer of $19 million or 9.5 times EBIT

When the sales process started, we believed that the probable value of the business was approximately 6 times EBIT, or $12 to $12.5 million. That is the range where we believed most of the offers would be, and we were correct, but we were selling without an asking price.

One buyer concluded that it could market the selling company's products in Europe and Asia through its sales organization, which would double the sales and profit in two years. That buyer determined that the business was worth more to them. The process forced them to offer as much as they could pay, because they didn't know who the other buyers were or what they would be willing to pay. That is why you sell without an asking price!

Let's look at another example.

In 1996 I sold a "small cap" NASDAQ public company by using the same selling technique. The difference between a private and a public company is that in the case of the public company, the market creates an asking price every day in the form of the market value of its shares. The current market price for a company's shares, however, is not measurably the same as the price that a buyer would have to pay in order to buy the entire company. This is because buyers understand that they will have to pay a premium over the current market price to acquire all of the shares. You may ask, "how much of a premium will they pay?" The answer is, "as much as you can extract out of them using the selling techniques that we are discussing."

In this example, the company's share price was $26 when I began discussions with the board of directors about representing them in a sale. The share price had risen to

$28 when the company announced that they had retained my firm to "maximize stockholder value." The share price increased during the sale process to $34, due to the speculation that always accompanies this kind of transaction. Because it was a public company, the buyers knew a great deal more about the business and its value than would normally be known in purchasing a private company. In the process of selling the company, I found 131 buyers interested in bidding on the company and sent informational memoranda to 59 of them. The informational memorandum contained no asking price, but included a request to make a bid.

Twelve buyers made offers to buy the company. The offers were received at a time when the market price of the stock was $36 per share. The buyers were told that we would sell to the highest bidder and that there would be only one round of bidding, but we actually intended to have a second round of bidding in order to maximize the price, and most of the buyers anticipated that this would happen.

The first round offers are listed in the following table:

First Round Offers from Competitive Auctioning Process			
Buyer	Offer in $/share	Buyer	Offer in $/share
Buyer 1	$47.50	Buyer 7	$39.94
Buyer 2	$44.38	Buyer 8	$39.94
Buyer 3	$44.00	Buyer 9	$36.98
Buyer 4	$40.00	Buyer 10	$36.98
Buyer 5	$40.00	Buyer 11	$35.50
Buyer 6	$39.94	Buyer 12	$34.00

Buyers 1, 2, and 3 were selected to bid in the second round. They were told that this was the final round and that the highest bidder would own the company. Here are the results of the second round.

	First Round Offer($/Share)	Second Round Offer($/Share)
Buyer 2	$44.38	$54.00
Buyer 3	$44.00	$49.00
Buyer 1	$47.50	$47.50

The company was sold to buyer 2 for $54 per share, or a 208 percent increase over the price of the shares when I began discussions with the board of directors of the company.

2. To sell for the highest price, contact as many buyers as possible.

There are some very important observations that can be made about this transaction, and those observations apply to any transaction that is sold through a competitive auctioning process. First, dealing with fewer buyers can result in a sale at less than full value. For example, if we had only contacted buyers 9, 10, 11, and 12, with what kind of deal would we have ended up? It is obvious that those buyers did not see the value in the business that the other buyers recognized.

The second and most important observation is that when you sell in a competitive auctioning process, *you force the buyers to put all of the money they are willing to spend on the table*. Keep in mind that this was a public company and we were going to sell it to the buyer who offered the highest price for the shareholders. Buyer 3 was the second highest bidder at $49 per share. Buyer 2 could have bought the company for $49.50 per share but didn't know that. But all the buyers knew they had to put all of the money they were willing to spend on the table because there would not be another chance to bid. Thus, bidding $48 per share and possibly not getting the company did not make sense. Because they wanted the company and could not risk underbidding, *they had to make their maximum offer.* Thus, they ended up paying $5 per share more than the second highest bidder, that price being the result of the secretive nature of the bidding process.

In a competitive auctioning process, bidders don't know who the other bidders are or what they are bidding.

3. What to say to buyers when they ask for a price.

The results of these transactions speak for themselves. You maximize value by selling without an asking price. Let the market determine the price. You will be thrilled with the results.

"OK, Steve," you say, "you convinced me — I am going to sell without an asking price. But how do I do it? Every buyer I talk to wants to know the price. How can I deal with buyers and not provide a price?"

Before I tell you how to do it, I must repeat the refrain that runs throughout this book. I am going to advise you on how to do it, but even if you completely understand the theory of what I am suggesting, it is very difficult to implement. In the real world, selling without an asking price and doing it effectively requires a tremendous amount of professional skill and experience in dealing with buyers. It requires the ability to manipulate their wants and desires to the advantage of the seller.

"OK," you say. "I understand all of that. Now, Steve, tell me, how do I sell without an asking price? My business is for sale. I am talking to an interested buyer who has signed a nondisclosure agreement and has been given financial and other information on my business. The buyer has read the material and he now calls me and says: 'Sam, I am interested in buying your company. What do you want for it?'"

Here is how you answer him: "I haven't put a price on the business, because it is possible that some buyers could see a value in the business that is greater than I think it could be. So, why should I prevent them from making a higher offer by stating a lower asking price? I am asking that you consider what you think the business is worth and make me your best offer. I am talking with several other buyers, and I have made similar requests of them. Whoever makes me the best offer buys the business. So put your best offer on the table, because I am not going to come back to you and ask for more." Of course, you always have the option of doing so, and it is highly recommended that you do come back and ask for more, because many buyers expect you to and so have not put their best offer on the table. While buyers don't like this approach, you can count on almost all of them to play along.

At the point that you have asked for bids, you have completely changed the leverage that exists in the normal buyer/seller relationship. The general rule is that the party who speaks first in regard to value is at a disadvantage.

Therefore, when the buyer makes a bid, you have the upper hand.

You may ask, what if the buyer won't play the game? Either I state a price or the buyer walks. This happens, and it is a great reason to make sure that you are being represented by an advisor with skill and experience in dealing with buyers, to get you through this kind of confrontation.

The most effective way to sell without an asking price is to deal with multiple buyers.

Dealing with multiple buyers gives you the ability to negotiate and leverage one buyer against another. An interesting characteristic of this process is that the buyers don't know what the price should be, and they don't know who the other players are. Thus, you can run a competitive bidding process without an asking price even while dealing with only one buyer. Running a competitive auction with only one buyer requires considerable skill, but an experienced mergers-and-acquisitions advisor can handle it

SECTION 3

The Sale Process — How it Works

The sale process begins when you decide to market your company. Once you make the decision to sell, the next step is to determine the sales strategy. There are four basic strategies that can be employed to effect the sale of a business. The positive and negative aspects of each of these strategies, along with my recommendations, are listed here.

Basic Sales Strategies

Strategy #1 – Exclusive Negotiations

An exclusive negotiation strategy exists when the business owner decides to negotiate with one buyer at a time for a limited time, until either an agreement is reached and the deal closes with that buyer, or it is determined that an agreement cannot be reached. Typically, a business owner would not back away from an exclusive negotiation unless the owner felt confident that all opportunities had been exhausted. When a business owner decides to approach a buyer on an exclusive basis, he or she believes that a particular buyer should buy the company. The seller, then, would have a significant level of commitment to the negotiations and would not withdraw until all avenues had been explored.

The big advantage of an exclusive negotiation is that dealing with only one buyer is a very discreet process, which substantially reduces the risk that there will be a breach of confidentiality to your employees, customers, and competitors. Giving information about your business to only one outsider instead of to numerous buyers limits the flow of information. Information given to one potential buyer can be further limited by linking the degree of thoroughness permitted in the "due diligence" investigation to your level of confidence in the buyer's ability to complete the deal. Another advantage of an exclusive negotiation is that it is normally more efficient than any of the other strategies. It provides the seller with a window of opportunity to reach a negotiated transaction, within a limited time frame, with a firm the seller believes is the most logical purchaser. Initial results can be assessed quickly. It is not unusual for this strategy to end in a closing several months after negotiations began.

I usually advise my clients to avoid the exclusive negotiation strategy because it has a number of negative attributes that make it unattractive. The biggest drawback is that the lack of competition almost always leads to a selling price that is substantially less than the business is worth. If you don't believe me, just ask the buyers. They know that a competitive process like an auction will drive up the price they will have to pay for a business. For this reason, buyers dislike participation in auctioning processes or in hybrid auctioning processes.

Another negative of the exclusive negotiation strategy is that it is only effective with buyers who have a great deal of interest in the business, a synergy with the business, and the financial ability to complete the deal. This strategy cannot be used with most financial buyers (who are a major force in the M&A market), because they normally lack the interest and synergy needed. Another problem is that this strategy doesn't guarantee a successful transaction. You could have exclusive negotiations over a period of time with a number of buyers in succession before you close a transaction with one of them. Thus, you could easily end up with a process in which you deal with a number of buyers without the competitive leverage produced by all of the other strategies.

I advise that you stay away from this strategy, because it will result in leaving millions of dollars on the table when you sell your business.

Strategy #2 – The Limited Auction

The "limited auction" strategy is employed in situations where a competitive process is desired with a limited number of interested buyers. You negotiate with the buyers at the same time, and select the preferred buyer for final negotiations on the basis of who is offering the highest price and providing the best terms and conditions. The advantage of this strategy is that it is a more discreet and expedient process than the traditional auction. At the same time, it is designed to promote competition among only the most interested parties. It is most effective when used with a very small pool of potential buyers.

The disadvantage of the limited auction is that it involves a very small pool of potential buyers. Given the current dynamic market in mergers and acquisitions, it is probable that this strategy will cause you to miss a number of potential buyers, any one of which could be the buyer who would pay the highest price for your business. While a limited auction usually provides superior results compared to an exclusive negotiation, it may not provide you with a vehicle to maximize the sale price.

Strategy #3 – The Traditional Auction

In the traditional auctioning strategy, a large number of potential purchasers are contacted. This strategy is similar to the limited auction in that you select the preferred buyer for final negotiations on the basis of which buyer offers to pay the highest price and provides the best terms and conditions. The major difference between the two strategies is that the traditional auction would result in a large number of participants being invited to submit final offers after participation in in-depth due diligence on the selling company. The advantage of this strategy is that it is a fair process to participants. In addition, it promotes the highest possible level of competition among buyers, thus creating an environment of maximum price potential. The disadvantage is that detailed information about the seller's company is distributed to many parties.

To provide a better understanding of how the traditional auctioning strategy works, the chart below lists the steps that would be followed in a traditional auction and in a limited auction. It also gives a cumulative amount of time estimated for each step. This process requires intensive management to assure that it moves smoothly and quickly to a closing.

Steps Followed by Most Investment Bankers in Managing the Auctioning Process		
Step		Week(s)
1.	Banker meets with senior management to discuss objectives of sale, including any special considerations such as tax motivation, off-balance-sheet liabilities, and owner-held assets not to be included.	0-1
2.	Representatives conduct due diligence on company and prepare confidential memorandum.	2-4
3.	Prepare list of prospective purchasers for discussion and obtain client's approval to approach buyers.	4
4.	Make initial contacts with prospective purchasers and obtain purchaser's confidentiality agreements.	5-7 5-7
5.	Request preliminary indications of value from prospective purchasers.	8
6.	Select five to six most likely buyers.	8
7.	Forward secondary materials on due diligence.	9-10
8.	Request further indications of value from prospective purchasers.	10
9.	Select three to four buyers for visits to the company and meetings with management.	11
10.	Provide additional due diligence to purchasers (document room).	11-12
11.	Deadline for final offers.	13
12.	Negotiate and execute letter of intent.	14-15
13.	Additional field due diligence by purchaser.	16-20
14.	Negotiate definitive purchase agreement.	20-24
15.	Transaction closes.	26

Strategy #4 – The Hybrid Process

This strategy combines parts of the previous three strategies. The seller contacts a significant number of potential purchasers and classifies them as priority one and priority two. Priority one buyers, those who have the highest level of interest, are contacted first. If their response is favorable, there may be no need to approach the priority two group. If the response from the priority one group is deemed to be insufficient, then the priority two group of buyers would immediately be contacted. The hybrid process is a competitive process that is not necessarily an auction. The process is flexible and would not preclude exclusive negotiations at any stage, or preclude consideration of a preemptive offer.

The advantage of the hybrid process is that it provides a significant level of competition with a potential for price-maximization, while still allowing the parties to opt for an exclusive negotiation at any point during the process. The major disadvantage is that it does not provide the seller with the same degree of leverage obtained from an auction. While it is a competitive process, the hybrid process probably will not result in as high a selling price as would be obtained from the auctioning process.

Conclusion

Ideally, the optimal strategy for the sale of a business should be determined in close consultation between the owner of the business and the mergers-and-acquisitions advisor. Factors to be considered include the number and nature of potential acquirers to be contacted, and the sensitivity of technological and other proprietary information to be disclosed. When fewer potential acquirers are expected and there is a high degree of sensitivity with respect to the disclosure of information, an exclusive negotiated sale may be more appropriate than competitive bidding.

BASIC SALES STRATEGIES
1. Exclusive negotiations (unadvisable)
2. Limited auction (small pool)
3. Traditional auction
4. Hybrid process

SECTION 4

Key Steps in the Sale Process

The sales process that will ultimately result in the sale of your business for the highest possible price has two main stages: (1) planning and preparation, and (2) implementation. Each of these stages has several steps that you and your mergers-and-acquisitions advisor will go through in consultation. As you read this section and look at the examples of related documents that I have provided in the Appendices, you will have a clear picture of the skills and experience that your M&A advisor will bring to the sales transaction.

Stage 1: Planning and Preparation

Step 1. Due diligence and memorandum of information.
The business owner and M&A advisor tour the facilities of the business and the owner begins the process of providing the advisor with greater detail about the business. The advisor gets the information needed to conduct a careful financial analysis of the business and assess its value. The key part of this first step is the drafting of a "sales presentation" memorandum, designed to be used as an effective marketing tool.

The memorandum of information is critical to the success of the sales process. The memorandum is the first impression of the business for potential acquirers. It will determine whether they have continuing interest in pursuing an acquisition of the company. Earlier I told you that "How To Sell Without an Asking Price" was the most important section in this book. While this is true, you cannot be effective using that technique unless you have interested buyers. The probability of generating interest from buyers is much higher with a well crafted memorandum of information. It should contain all of the essential information on products, customers, industry, marketing, management, equipment, and facilities that a buyer would need to make an offer on the company.

The M&A advisor can write a superb memorandum of information as a result of extensive due diligence investigating. Due diligence is critical because: (1) it requires the writer to provide an independent perspective on the business; (2) it helps the advisor understand the strengths and weaknesses of the business and how to play up the strengths and play down its weaknesses; (3) and it provides the advisor with insights that can avoid unpleasant surprises later in the sales process.

Essentially, mergers-and-acquisitions advisors are in the sales business. In sales, the more you know about the product you are selling, the more successful you will be in the selling of that product. That statement also applies to the sale of a business.

Thorough due diligence gives the advisor the knowledge that is needed to sell for the highest price possible.

Over the years, I have developed and refined my checklist for providing due diligence. The comprehensive checklist is included as Appendix A. It covers all aspects of the business being sold. Completing this checklist should provide all of the necessary information to write an effective memorandum of information.

Appendix B contains an example of a memorandum of information. This memorandum resulted from a comprehensive effort in due diligence. When you read this memorandum, notice the level of detail. Then you will understand why thorough due diligence is an absolute necessity. The executive summary is the most important part of the memorandum, and it must contain a hook. Potential buyers will read the executive summary first. If it catches their interest, they will they go on to read the rest of the document.

The executive summary contains a snapshot of the business and spells out why the buyer should be interested. The most important part of the executive summary is the "investment highlights." I spend a substantial amount of time developing and articulating creative and compelling investment highlights. Read the investment highlights in the sample memorandum and you will see that they clearly articulate why a buyer should be interested in this deal. Most important, writing compelling investment highlights substantially improves the probability that a potential buyer will read the entire memorandum and become interested in pursuing the deal.

Carefully read the sample memorandum. It will provide you with insight into the kinds of information you will have to provide when you sell your company.

Step 2. Valuation.
The planning part of the sale process includes a full analysis of valuation conducted by the M&A advisor. This analysis should include an analysis of comparable public companies, acquisitions of similar companies, and a valuation based upon discounted cash flow. This valuation is useful for evaluating offers from buyers.

Step 3. Search for buyers.
The final part of the planning stage entails in-depth research to analyze the universe of potential acquirers and identify the key candidates.

Stage 2: Implementation

Step 1. Approach potential buyers/identify the most interested parties.
Identification of potential buyers is a collaborative effort. After an initial list is developed by the advisor, the owner reviews it, adds or deletes names, and approves the final list. Potential buyers that are approved by the owner of the

business are then contacted by the M&A advisor. The contacts are usually made according to a precise timetable, and the interest of these potential buyers is assessed. Interested buyers, with proven financial capability, are then sent the memorandum of information after signing an appropriate agreement regarding nondisclosure and confidentiality. After reviewing the memorandum, buyers are asked to provide an indication of the value they place on the company and a proposed structure for a transaction.

Step 2. Discussion and presentation by management to potential buyers, and buyers' evaluations.

The next step in the process narrows down the prospective buyers on the basis of the value that they place on the company. A limited number of financially qualified buyers — those who see the highest value in the business — are selected for meetings with management. This is usually in the range of six to eight buyers. At a series of meetings, managers of the company make presentations to the potential buyers, discussing the business and its potential. These meetings also provide an opportunity for discussions of areas of interest or concern to the potential buyers. Additional information is made available to the buyers to allow them to conduct their own evaluation prior to making a formal offer. If an auctioning strategy is being employed, it is usually appropriate to receive such offers on a designated date.

Step 3. Receipt of offers, negotiations, and selection of buyer.

The owner of the business reviews the offers with the M&A advisor, analyzing the key points in finance and business terms contained in each offer. The owner relies on the advisor to help clear up any other issues that need to be discussed with the prospective buyers. Negotiations then commence, with the prospective buyers submitting their best offers, and the competitive auctioning process (or one of the other strategies) determines the selection of a buyer.

Step 4. Buyer's due diligence and negotiation of a purchase and sale agreement.

Once a decision is made to proceed with a specific buyer, the seller's attorney, working in partnership with the M&A advisor, will negotiate all of the legal aspects of the agreement. At the same time, the buyer's representatives will engage in a thorough due diligence investigation in order to verify all facts and representations made to the buyer throughout the selling process.

Step 5. Closing of the transaction.
After an agreement is reached and a formal document is signed, there may be additional procedures required prior to closing, such as final legal and other due diligence, and resolution of any problems that may arise. The entire sales process typically takes from six to nine months to complete.

KEY STEPS
- **Planning and preparation**
  1. **Due diligence, memorandum of information**
  2. **Valuation**
  3. **Search for buyers**

- **Implementation**
  1. **Identification of and approach to interested parties**
  2. **Presentation by managers to potential buyers, buyers' evaluations**
  3. **Receipt of offers, negotiation, selection**
  4. **Buyer's due diligence and negotiation**
  5. **Closing**

SECTION 5

How Deals Are Structured

I have never met a business owner who did not want an all-cash deal, and fortunately, I am usually able to provide my clients with the deal they desire. But getting an all-cash deal is not something you can take for granted. In sales of private companies, all-cash deals are the exception rather than the rule. The reason for my track record is that I have been able to locate "strategic buyers" for my clients' companies. Strategic buyers normally do not have to depend on financing individual transactions to secure the funds for purchase. Such buyers normally have the ability to write a check for whatever businesses they purchase.

At any given time there are very few strategic buyers in the market. In addition, strategic buyers are very selective about which transactions they pursue. These buyers are difficult to contact and even more difficult to interest in any given transaction. In most instances, only skilled mergers-and-acquisitions intermediaries have the contacts to deal with a number of strategic buyers. If you want to sell to a strategic buyer, you should be represented by one of these intermediaries.

Without an all-cash deal, most deals are structured in order to achieve the desired sale price. The major factor inhibiting all-cash deals is the low net worth of most privately held businesses compared to the expected selling price. This condition makes it difficult for the nonstrategic buyer to obtain outside financing sufficient to provide for an all-cash purchasing price. If an all-cash deal is not possible, buyers normally expect sellers to accept deferred compensation or to take a continued financial interest in the business using vehicles such as notes, covenant-not-to-compete payments, and earnouts. Some combination of these vehicles will be used to make up the difference between what can be financed and the agreed-on selling price. It is important for you as the seller to understand the components of these types of structures for a deal in order to achieve the best possible structure for your transaction.

As you review the information that follows, keep in mind that the structure of a deal tends to be tailor-made for the transaction. Most transactions will contain appropriate components that fit the deal. A transaction will rarely contain all of these components. The following are typical components used in structured transactions:

Cash. Typically in a structured transaction, the amount of cash available to the seller is limited by two factors: (1) the amount of equity the buyer plans to put into the deal, and (2) the amount of financing that the buyer can obtain to purchase the company. Financing is normally secured from asset-based senior lenders whose loans are predicated upon given percentages of the acquired company's receivables, inventory, and fixed assets. In some transactions, "mezzanine" or subordinate lenders are utilized to supplement the funds provided by the senior lenders. "Mezzanine" lenders usually base their loans on the cash flow of the company and their funds can be used to bridge the gap in providing more cash to the seller in transactions where the sale price is substantially greater than the net worth of the selling company. In smaller middle-market transactions, it is difficult to find sources of mezzanine financing. Experienced mergers-and-acquisitions professionals know the sources of mezzanine financing and should be called upon to determine whether this type of financing is available.

Subordinated Notes. Typically these notes are not guaranteed by the buyer and are secured by the assets of the company being sold. The interest rate paid, the term, schedule of repayment, and whether the notes will be partially or wholly guaranteed are all part of the negotiation process.

Retained Ownership of Stock. A continuing ownership of stock is common in those deals where the seller plans to remain with the company for a significant period of time after the sale. But unless the seller negotiates for a right to put the stock back to the company, there is no guarantee that sale of the retained shares will result in obtaining complete liquidity.

Non-Compete Agreements. You should be prepared to provide the buyer with a commitment that after the sale, you will not compete in any way with the business being sold. Non-compete agreements vary in their terms. The typical term is five years. In every transaction the buyer will allocate a portion of the purchasing price to the non-compete agreement. In an all-cash deal, the portion of the purchasing price allocated to the non-compete agreement is typically paid to the seller at closing. In a structured transaction, the amount allocated to the non-compete agreement is typically paid over the term of the non-compete agreement.

Consulting/Employment Agreements. In transactions where the selling shareholders are either leaving the company or reducing their involvement after the sale, part of the purchasing price is allocated to long-term (usually three to five years) agreements for consulting or employment of such selling stockholders. Buyers like to allocate as much as possible to such agreements, because these payments are tax deductible.

Earnouts. Earnouts are rights acquired by the seller to share in future earnings of the company. Earnout agreements typically run for three to five years after the sale. Earnouts most frequently occur in transactions where the seller remains as the manager of the business. The rationale behind earnout agreements is that the potential payments motivate selling shareholders to continue to perform after the sale. Earnouts can provide selling shareholders with significant additional value, but in practice they are difficult to realize because of the requirement to exceed the high threshold levels of profits specified in most earnout agreements.

Royalties. Royalties are rights to receive specific payments over a period of years. Most royalty agreements are given to selling shareholders of companies that have proprietary technology, patents, trademarks, or brand names created by the seller that have substantial ongoing value. Royalty payments are normally reflected as a percentage of sales. Unlike earnouts, royalties can be paid regardless of earnings of the company, unless such agreements have thresholds of profits that limit payments.

Structures of most deals will contain part or all of the elements listed here. As a seller, you need to determine which of these elements is preferable over others. After receiving the cash portion of the deal, your ability to be paid from each of the other elements is totally dependent on the continued success of the business. Recognizing the contingent nature of all structured payments, your negotiations should attempt to create as much certainty as possible in receiving the structured portion of the deal.

You create certainty by negotiating as much of the structured value as possible into subordinated notes, non-compete agreements, and consulting/ employment payments instead of earnouts. Holding notes, even though subordinated to senior lenders, makes you a creditor with a potential claim on the company's assets. Also, notes create certainty in regard to the amount of the payment, provided the business continues to be successful.

Certain forms of payments such as notes, non-competition payments, and consulting/employment payments are preferred over earnouts. Those forms contain certainty in the amount to be paid to the seller, while earnouts may never be paid, even though the business continues to be able to pay its notes, non-compete agreements, and employment agreements.

HOW DEALS ARE STRUCTURED
- Cash
- Subordinated notes
- Retained stock-ownership
- Non-compete agreements
- Consulting/employment agreements
- Earnouts
- Royalties

SECTION 6

The Most Common Structures for Deals and How I Rate Those Structures

Imagine that you are the owner of Global Precision Manufacturing Company. The company produces precision parts for the automotive and aerospace industries. You founded the company 30 years ago when you were 35 years old. The business has prospered over those 30 years, and its future outlook is bright. You have no family members in the business, and none of your children are interested in participating. Due to your age and your desire to retire, you have now decided to sell.

Your company's historical and projected statements of income and balance sheets at the time of sale are shown below.

Statement of Income for Global Precision Manufacturing Company					
	Prior Yr 1	Prior Yr 2	Sale Year	Projected Yr 1	Projected Yr 2
Sales	$23,000,000	$25,500,000	$28,000,000	$32,000,000	$35,000,000
Cost of Sales	13,800,000	15,300,000	16,800,000	19,200,000	21,000,000
Gross Profit	9,200,000	10,200,000	11,200,000	12,800,000	14,000,000
Selling/ Admin.	4,600,000	5,100,000	5,600,000	6,400,000	7,000,000
Operat- ing Profit	4,600,000	5,100,000	5,600,000	6,400,000	7,000,000

Balance Sheet for Global Precision Manufacturing Company	
Current Assets:	**Current Liabilities:**
Cash $3,000,000	Accounts Payable $2,500,000
Accounts Receivable $4,000,000	Other Current $1,000,000
Inventory $5,000,000	Total Current Liabilities $3,500,000
Misc. Assets $500,000	Long Term Liabilities:
Total Current Assets $12,500,000	Stockholder Equity $15,000,000
Fixed Assets:	Total Liability & Equity $18,500,000
Net Fixed Assets $6,000,000	
Total Assets $18,500.000	

Your company has been for sale for five months, and you have received seven offers to purchase your business. Each offer contains a differently structured deal. These offers and the structures of their deals are summarized below in the order of their recommended desirability.

Offer 1. Sale of 100% of the assets or stock of your business for $40 million cash.

Offer 2. Sale of 100% of the stock of your business for $40 million in stock of a publicly traded company.

Offer 3. Sale of 75% of the stock of your company for $33 million cash. You have a put and the purchaser has a call to cause the balance of the stock to be sold at the end of three years at a value of six times last year's trailing EBIT.

Offer 4. Sale of 100% of the assets or stock of your business for $35 million in cash in a leveraged transaction where you reinvest $5 million with a financial buyer for 50% of the stock in the company you sold.

Offer 5. Sale of 100% of the assets or stock of your business for $30 million in cash, plus a $15 million, eight-year subordinated note using your company as collateral payable to the seller (interest only, until maturity), paying 8% interest annually.

Offer 6. Sale of 100% of the assets or stock of your business for $30 million cash, plus a $10 million, eight-year subordinated note (interest only until maturity) paying 8% interest annually, and an earnout equal to 50% of the annual operating profit in excess of $5.6 million for the next five years (projected value $8 million).

Offer 7. Sale of 100% of the assets or stock of your business for $32 million in cash and an earnout equal to 100% of the annual operating profit in excess of $5 million for the next five years (projected value $16 million).

Each of these offers is based on a differently structured deal that creates a different potential value for the seller. Now I will examine each of these offers, explain how they work, why buyers use them, and how I would rate them in desirability. While there are numerous other potential structures for deals that buyers use to purchase businesses, those we will examine represent the most common types of proposals, which account for 95% or more of the deals being done in the United States.

Offer 1. Sale of 100% of assets or stock of your company for $40 million cash.

This is definitely the most desirable transaction for the seller, because it is an all-cash deal. Notwithstanding anything you may have seen or heard to the contrary, cash is king and *nothing* beats an all-cash deal. "OK, Steve," you say, "an all-cash deal is at the top of the food chain, but I have a friend who sold his company to Byron Technologies, and he took back shares in that public company. Two years later his shares have increased in value by 250%! Look at all the extra money he made by taking stock instead of cash. Do you still believe that all-cash is the best way to go?"

My answer is without question, "Yes." The all-cash deal is the best deal for any seller. Remember: For every seller who takes stock in a public company and has a positive experience with the value of those shares increasing, there are many more who have suffered losses with their public shares before they could sell them.

Selling a business for cash can be accomplished in two kinds of trans-actions — either a stock sale or an asset sale. A stock sale would take place if you sold 100% of the shares you own in Global Precision to the purchas-er, who gives you cash. Such a transaction would be analogous to your sell-ing 1000 shares of General Motors on the New York Stock Exchange. You would receive cash; the purchaser would receive the GM shares and would then step into the identical position of ownership you had before you sold them. That explanation is rather simplistic, however, since you are selling shares in a private rather than a public company. This is an area that lawyers enjoy writing volumes about, so I will leave the details to them and just touch briefly on the key issues.

Sales of stock compared to sales of assets. A sale of stock of a private company offers a number of important benefits to a seller. In fact, I would describe sales of stock as seller-friendly. Buyers usually prefer sales of assets, but sales of stock are much easier to consummate than sales of assets. I won't go into the details of why they are easier, but if you're inter-ested, you can get a complete explanation from your attorney. My message is that it is much easier and simpler to transfer the stock of a company than it is to transfer all of its assets. Consequently, a sale of stock should result in lower legal costs for the seller than would be incurred if the transaction were a sale of assets.

A sale of stock has another important advantage over a sale of assets. All liabilities from any unknown or unforeseen problems that may arise in the future would belong to the purchaser. In a sale of assets, the seller would retain the corporate shell and would have ultimate responsibility for such problems. Purchasers of stock will attempt to mitigate their risk of unfore-seen liabilities through representations and warranties in the purchase-and-sale agreement, but those representations and warranties do not cover all of the possible future adverse events that could occur. Even if the events were covered, the representations and warranties typically survive the closing by only one to two years. After that period, a seller of stock has no further lia-bility or responsibility to the purchaser.

Perhaps the most important reason that sellers want to complete sales of stock is taxes. If you own a "C" corporation, for purposes of the federal income tax, you will have a double impact of taxation on the sale if you sell the assets of the company. If you have an "S" corporation, for purposes of federal income tax, it is possible to sell assets without the impact of double taxation, but it is not unusual for "S" corporations also to have certain tax problems. Thus, it is important for you to discuss the tax ramifications of sales of assets compared to sales of stock, with your tax advisor. Have your tax advisor compute the cost of a sale of assets in advance of your taking the company into the market. The issue is certain to be brought up by buyers. If your only alternative to get a deal done is a sale of assets, you had better be educated on the tax ramifications long before you have to deal with it.

If sales of stock are seller-friendly, then sales of assets are just the opposite. Buyers love sales of assets. Why? There are two main reasons. First, sales of assets limit the liability and exposure that a buyer assumes. The buyer is buying only the operating assets of the business and certain agreed upon liabilities. All of the other liabilities of that business, whether actual or contingent, remain with the seller. Remember, in the sale of stock the exposure of the purchaser to post-sale liabilities is much greater.

The second and most important reason that buyers want sales of assets is taxes. That's right — taxes! What's bad for the seller's taxes happens to be good for the buyer's. In sales of assets, buyers can allocate almost all of the purchasing price to assets — including goodwill — that can be depreciated or amortized for purposes of federal income tax. Therefore, in most sales of assets, buyers can recover 34 to 40 percent (depending on state tax rates) of their original purchasing price through tax deductions over a maximum of 15 years after the purchase closes.

Sellers normally want sales of stock. Buyers normally want sales of assets. As a seller, what should you do? The answer is — always strive for an all-cash stock deal, be informed, and be represented by a competent, knowledgeable advisor.

Offer 2. Sale of 100% of the stock of your business for $40 million in stock of a publicly traded company.
Stock-for-stock transactions occur for three primary reasons:
    1.A number of public companies have shares that sell for a very high

price-earnings (P.E.) multiple, and such companies, as a matter of policy, only use stock in making acquisitions. Such acquisitions tend to be accretive to earnings per share of the public acquirer, because the price paid as a multiple of earnings is significantly less than the P.E. of the public stock given to the seller.

2. Public companies offering stock with high P.E. multiples can, and often do, offer to buy businesses for prices that substantially exceed all-cash offers. Thus, sellers opt for the stock-for-stock deal.

3. Many stock-for-stock deals occur because of the seller's desire to defer taxes on capital gains. In a stock-for-stock deal, taxes on capital gains are paid only when the newly acquired stock is sold.

On the surface, it would appear that the sale of your business for $40 million in stock in a publicly traded company is similar to a sale for $40 million in cash, with the only difference being that taxes on capital gains are deferred until the shares are sold. You're thinking, "This is a public company, and there is a market for this stock. Therefore, any time I want to sell it and turn it into $40 million, I can." That statement would be true if the market price of the stock never changed and there were no restrictions on your ability to sell your shares. Prices of stock go up and down, however, and that market risk is the major drawback to doing stock-deals. In addition, in most stock-for-stock deals, the public company places restrictions on the sellers' ability to sell its shares. Such restrictions, which last from one to two years, generally prohibit all sales during the restricted period. Consequently you would be totally exposed to negative market reaction to the stock during that time, and unable to sell shares.

Here is an example of how one of my clients was negatively impacted by restrictions in a stock-for-stock transaction.

In the mid-'90's, I sold a very profitable consumer products manufacturer for $75 million to a large ($1.5 billion in sales) blue-chip New York Stock Exchange company in a stock-for-stock transaction. Before they agreed to do the deal, I exhaustively reviewed with my clients the risks of taking so much stock in one public company. My clients could have opted for an all-cash deal, but they decided to proceed with the stock deal because (a) they had almost no basis in their stock and wanted to defer taxes on capital gains, and (b) they felt that the company they were selling to was a quality company, and they felt comfortable owning its shares.

The shares that my clients received in this public company contained restrictions that prohibited their sale until two years after the closing. Shortly after the closing, the research departments of two large securities firms' downgraded their ratings in the public company. In addition, in the next quarter the company's earnings declined significantly. Hearing the bad news, my clients wanted to sell but couldn't. They were locked in for two years. One year after the transaction closed, the shares that my clients held in this public company were worth 40% less than the value they got at the closing. You have to admit that 40% is an awfully large discount to give in order to defer capital gains taxes on the sale.

In a transaction in which my clients believed they were maximizing value and selling for a very high price, they ended up with a value that they never would have sold for in the first place. If they had sold for $75 million in cash, their after-tax proceeds would have been substantially higher than the current market value of their public shares. Furthermore, the value would be further reduced by capital gains taxes when the shares were sold. There are lots of horror stories out there about entrepreneurs who suffered major post-closing losses in market value in stock-for-stock deals. There are also many stories about entrepreneurs who made additional profits in the stock they acquired. I represented a client who sold his hardware manufacturing company to a large public company. The client never sold the shares, which are now worth ten times more than the value received at the time he sold his company.

In conclusion, I will offer you the same advice I give to every client considering a stock-for-stock deal. First, a stock-for-stock deal should not be driven by considerations of taxes. Adverse market conditions can easily wipe out the 20% federal tax deferral achieved in such transactions. The most important considerations are the investment aspects of the stock you are acquiring. Ask yourself, if you had $75 million to invest, would you invest it all in the stock of this company? If the answer is "no," then you should not engage in a stock-for-stock swap with that company. A stock-for-stock swap is analogous to a purchase, for investment purposes, of $75 million of the shares of that public company.

Stock-for-stock transactions have their advantages, but I believe nothing is better than an all-cash deal.

Offer 3. Sale of 75% of the stock of your business for $33 million cash. In addition, you have a put and the purchaser has a call to cause the balance of the stock to be sold at the end of three years at a value of six times last year's trailing EBIT, or a projected $12 million. Total projected value of the deal — $45 million.

Here is how the structure of this deal works. At the closing, you receive $33 million in cash for 75% of the stock. In addition, you will sign a managerial contract to continue to manage the business for the next three years. At the end of the three-year period, you have the right to sell the remaining shares to the purchaser at a value of six times the last full year's EBIT. At the same time, the purchaser also has an option to acquire the shares for the same price. The purpose of puts and calls is to assure the parties that the balance of the shares will be acquired.

This is a very common structure for deals offered by buyers and is often used by public companies as an incentive for sellers to maximize the performance of the business in the period following the sale. I have had four different clients who have sold their businesses to public companies using variations of this structure for the deal. Forcing you to retain 25% of the stock with its value dependent on future profits gives buyers comfort that you will remain dedicated and motivated in the management of the business. The value of the shares that you will sell in the future will depend upon your ability to manage and grow the profits over a three-year period. Thus, you remain at substantial risk concerning the value of your remaining stock.

This structure for a deal is normally considered to be buyer-friendly, because it shifts the risk of future performance to the seller. If the business does not perform, you will receive reduced value in the purchasing price for the retained shares. Another way to view this transaction from a buyer's viewpoint is that the cash value of the business is $40 million, but by giving $33 million cash and a structured future payout the buyer has achieved a $33 million purchase price if the business does not perform in the future. It is noteworthy that the buyer in this transaction has committed to pay more than

$40 million in value for the business if you excel in management of future profits. My experience is, however, that sellers rarely obtain the additional value of that purchase price under such arrangements.

This type of structure for a deal is not as desirable as either an all-cash or a stock-for-stock deal. The reason is that only $33 million of the purchasing price is guaranteed. Thus, you assume the risk of future performance in order to obtain the balance of the selling price. The selling price in both the all-cash sale and the stock-for-stock sale is never contingent on future performance. Sellers accept this kind of structure for a deal mainly because it represents the best deal available, which means that it would have more value than the best all-cash offer on the table.

An example of how this structure works is the Redwood Industries transaction I closed in 1997.

> Redwood was an industrial product manufacturer that I sold to a New York Stock Exchange company. My clients received $15 million in cash for 75% of the stock in their company. There were puts and calls on the balance of the shares at the end of three years, at seven times EBIT. I had negotiated a floor on the value of the remaining shares at $5 million, which guaranteed my clients at least $20 million, the value that they wanted for their company. There was also a $15 million cap on the value of the remaining shares.
>
> The reason my clients accepted this offer was that their next best offer was an all-cash deal for $16 million. The deal we accepted had guaranteed cash of $20 million. Even with its structure and future risk it was clearly the best deal to take.

Structures of this nature for proposed deals have to be evaluated in comparison to all the other offers. Take the best deal on the table, and if this kind of deal is the best one available — take it!

Offer 4. Sale of 100% of the assets or stock of your business for $35 million cash in a leveraged transaction where you reinvest $5 million with a financial buyer for a 50% stock interest in the company you sold.

This type of structure for a deal is often referred to as a leveraged recapitalization of the business. Here is how this structure works. The buyer, a financial buying group, forms a new company, "New Co." The capitalization for New Co. is as follows: Equity, $10 million; senior debt, $20 million, and mezzanine or subordinated debt, $8 million, for a total capitalization of $38 million.

New Co. then acquires 100% of the stock of Global Precision for $35 million in cash, and then merges itself into Global Precision. To the outside world the transaction is invisible. You take $5 million of $35 million in cash proceeds and reinvest the funds for a 50% stake in the newly leveraged Global Precision. The $30 million in proceeds you take off of the table is made available by the leverage that has been placed upon the business with $28 million in new credit facilities. Twenty-five million dollars of the new credit facilities are used to pay off the seller, with the balance going into working capital. The remaining $5 million that is paid to you comes from the financial buying group that now becomes your partner. When the smoke clears after the deal is done, you will have $30 million in cash (for a business that you believe is worth $40 million in cash) and a continuing interest in your business, but it is now encumbered with substantial debt.

The goal of the financial buying group facilitating the deal is to make a substantial (35 to 40 percent) annual return on their $5 million investment and obtain liquidity in five to seven years. Liquidity for the financial buyers would take place under one of three scenarios: (1) you sell the company again to a third party, (2) you take the company public, (3) the company continues to grow and reduces its debt with its annual cash flows and then, in five to seven years, refinances itself using a new credit facility to purchase the shares held by the financial buying group. In the third scenario, the repurchase would provide you with 100% of the ownership again. So, if everything goes according to plan, you could take out $30 million in cash, which would be taxed at capital gains rates, and in five to seven years or less, you could regain 100% control of the company.

The leveraged recapitalization structure for a deal has unique characteristics that appeal only to certain business owners. You would consider engaging in this type of transaction when you do not want to engage in an outright sale of your company. You would prefer to stay with the business and control its ownership and destiny and possibly pass the ownership on to your heirs. At the same time, as a good businessperson who is getting older, you recognize the existence of significant financial risks in having all of your net worth tied up in the business. This type of deal allows you to take some chips off the table and still continue to own and control the business. The $30 million cash payout from the recapitalization substantially reduces your risk. On the other hand, it is important to point out that this kind of transaction greatly magnifies the risk of future business failure because of the substantial debt load that has been placed on the business.

In this case, the partners took a business with no debt and increased its structure of debt by $28 million. Such credit facilities contain provisions for payments of interest and principal, along with covenants relating to the financial performance of the business. If business conditions deteriorate, resulting in the business being unable to abide by the terms of its lending agreement, the lender would call its loan and put the future of the business in jeopardy. You now have $30 million in chips off the table, but the future of the business will exist in a precarious debt-laden environment.

The risk created by the large amount of new debt is the major drawback to this kind of transaction. Nevertheless, I frequently use this kind of transaction to satisfy the needs of my clients. If you are not a seller, but want to take some chips off the table, this transaction could work for you. On the other hand, a leveraged recapitalization would not be right for the business owner whose main goal is to sell for the highest price and retire.

A leveraged recapitalization is not a pure sale. Typically, valuations for leveraged recapitalizations are *below* the valuations that could be achieved in competitive auctioning type of sales.

Offer 5. Sale of 100% of the assets or stock of your business for $30 million cash, plus a $15 million, eight-year subordinated note based on your business as collateral (interest only, until maturity) paying 8% interest annually.
At first blush, this looks like a $45 million deal, but only $30 million is guaranteed, and payout of the $15 million note is subject to substantial future

risk. Here is how the structure of this deal works. At the closing you receive $30 million in cash and a note for $15 million. The note has an eight-year term, and pays 8% interest per year, but no payments of principal are due until maturity. This type of note, usually referred to as seller-financing, is subordinated to all bank debt, and the buyers that issue them seldom guarantee such notes. Thus, the only way that you can receive payment at maturity is if the business continues to prosper and is able to pay off the note in eight years. These notes carry a high degree of risk. Usually in these deals there would be a significant amount of senior bank debt secured by all of the assets of the business. The seller's notes would have no assets to secure them and really represent a de facto form of equity supporting the buyer's purchase.

With only $30 million or 2/3 of the purchase price guaranteed and the balance at risk, you might question why you would ever accept such a deal. The answer is simple. It was the best deal you were offered. Even though it had risk, it was superior to the other alternatives. This kind of structure is typically offered by buyers for one or more of the following three reasons:
1. The buyer is unable or unwilling to put enough equity into the deal to cash out the seller completely.
2. The buyer is unable to secure enough financing for the acquisition, which, coupled with the investment of equity, is insufficient to cash out the seller totally.
3. The buyer uses the seller's note to hedge the risk on 1/3 of the purchase price. The buyer's risk is limited to the $30 million cash portion of the purchasing price. The balance of the purchasing price, $15 million, is not paid by the buyer, but instead is paid out of the future cash flow of the business. If the business is successful over the next eight years, the seller gets a total of $45 million. If the business is not successful, the seller could receive substantially less than the $15 million due on the note.

Obviously, this is not the most desirable kind of structure for a deal, but if this kind of structure is the best alternative offered to you, before you agree to it, try to incorporate some of the following suggested changes which will increase the odds of your eventual payout. Try to get some form of security to back up your note. If the buyer refuses to give you a blanket guarantee, try to get a partial guarantee. Perhaps you can prevail upon the buyer to give you a letter of credit to secure part or all of your note.

If guarantees of any form are not available, you can still reduce your risk by negotiating a shorter term on the note. For example, try to get a five-year instead of an eight-year term, or negotiate for an amortizing note instead of a balloon payout. Your risk will be reduced as amortization of the note begins. Remember, the longer you wait for payment, the greater your risk in receiving it.

Offer 6. Sale of 100% of the assets or stock of your business for $30 million cash, plus a $10 million, eight-year subordinated note (interest only until maturity), paying 8% interest annually, and an earnout equal to 50% of the annual operating profit in excess of $5.6 million for the next five years (projected earnout value $8 million).

As a non-financial person reading this book, you could easily conclude that this is the best deal that we have discussed so far because it is worth a projected $48 million. You will recall, however, that earlier I said I would be listing these deals in order of their recommended desirability. Thus, you can conclude that I do not believe that this kind of transaction offers a seller as much potential as the other five structures for a deal that have been discussed.

The main difference between this deal and Offer #5 is that this deal contains a smaller note ($10 million rather than $15 million), and the $5 million reduction in the note is replaced by an earnout with a projected value of $8 million. The earnout could be defined as that part of the purchasing price that is achieved by the seller only when future earnings of the business exceed certain established threshold levels, such as 50% of the operating profit in excess of $5.6 million for five years.

As already noted, seller's notes contain a great deal of risk, but the odds that seller's notes will be paid are much greater than the odds of receiving payments from an earnout. In the deal we are discussing, you would be much better off in negotiating an additional $5 million in notes and giving up the right to the earnout, because my experience has been that sellers seldom receive much value out of the earnout portion of a deal. There are a number of reasons why earnouts produce little value. The two most significant reasons are:

1. Lack of control. No matter what the buyer says or promises before the sale, the fact remains that after the sale the buyer, not the seller, controls the business. This makes it more difficult for the seller to achieve the results needed to cause the earnout to pay off.

2. Perhaps the most important reason that earnouts seldom pay off is that most entrepreneurs know when their business is peaking and that is when they sell. Therefore, if you sell at the peak it would be difficult to achieve the aggressive projections buyers use to cause earnouts to pay off.

Sellers' notes are risky, but are always better than an earnout. Earnouts seldom pay off, so always try to avoid them when you negotiate your deal.

Offer 7. Sale of 100% of the assets or stock of your business for $32 million in cash and an earnout equal to 100% of the annual operating profit in excess of $5.6 million for the next five years (projected value $16 million).

This is the worst choice among all of the structures offered, because one-third of the projected price of the sale is in the form of an earnout. Remember what I said earlier — my experience is that sellers seldom receive much value out of the earnout portion of a deal. In reviewing this deal, there is a high probability that you would wind up with only $32 million in cash as the proceeds received from the sale. Therefore, as a seller you would only agree to this structure for a deal if you were willing to accept $32 million as the minimum price for which you would be willing to sell your business.

Conclusion

When the time comes to sell your business you will, in all probability, be presented with a number of different offers and structures for deals to review. As you review these deals, keep in mind that the most critical element in each deal is certainty of payment. In this example, you spent 30 years building your business, and now you are selling it for $40 million. You want to make sure that the deal you accept has the certainty in its structure to provide you with that $40 million.

Not every business is sold through an all-cash deal. If an all-cash deal is not available to you, then negotiate a structure for a deal with as much certainty as possible in the chances of receiving future payments. Avoid earnouts, if you can. They seldom pay off.

> **Only an all-cash deal can provide you with certainty of payment. *All other* structures offer certain risks that could affect the ultimate payment you would receive.**

SECTION 7

The Final Message

In February, 1990, a call came in to the switchboard operator at our firm. The caller told the operator he was contemplating the sale of his business and wanted to speak to one of the managing directors. The call was transferred to me, since I was the only managing director who was not at lunch. I picked up the phone, and the caller introduced himself as William Talburt, president of Advanced Cooking Technologies of Indianapolis, Indiana. He told me his company invented, manufactured, and sold patented cooking devices that were manufactured with proprietary technology. He was interested in discussing the sale of his business and wanted to meet with me at McCormick Place, where he was showing his products at the Housewares Show.

A cab ride that afternoon to McCormick Place began a four-year relationship with William Talburt. We met at his booth; he demonstrated his products, and then we walked the exhibition hall to examine the booths of his competitors. My observation was that none of his competitors were offering products like those of Advanced Cooking Technologies. Talburt's company had patent protection and perhaps two years to develop the market for these unique items before the other players would have competitive products in the market.

At the conclusion of our meeting, Talburt asked me to visit his factory in Indianapolis and meet his two partners, which I did the following week. That visit convinced me that Advanced Cooking Technologies had several unique and wonderful products which, in the right hands, could generate huge sales. The owners appeared to be entrepreneurs who were outstanding in conceptualizing and developing unique new products, but they lacked the experience needed for large-scale quality production of such products, and they lacked the customer-penetration necessary to move their products quickly into consumers' channels. The housewares industry is a faddish business where new and unusual products sell in enormous quantities and exclusivity seldom lasts long, because competitors quickly copy new products, causing sales and margins to decline.

For the year ended March 31, 1990, Advanced Cooking Technologies had sales of $8 million and pretax profit of $450,000. Little was known in the industry about the company and its products, but the company had succeeded in obtaining placement of its products in Wal-Mart and Target, as well as several other chains. We agreed to commence the sale process for the company in the third quarter of 1991. There were a number of reasons why that was the perfect time to sell this business.

First, with its new placements with customers, 1991 would be an excellent year for sales and profit, but almost all of the future sales for these products would be after 1991. Thus, large players such as Panasonic, Sunbeam, Black & Decker, National Presto, Sanyo, Sony, and so on, could purchase the company, place their brand onto Advanced Cooking Technologies' products, and have almost all of the life cycle of the new products in sales available to them. Furthermore, these large players sold to every retailer in the U.S. and were assured of instant placement of these new products, while on its own, Advanced would never achieve anywhere near that level of penetration to customers. In addition, Advanced was not an efficient quality manufacturer of these products, while bigger players in the industry could manufacture products of higher quality at much lower cost. Thus, the products would be much more profitable to them than they ever could be to Advanced.

Finally, and most important, we did not believe that there would be any competitive products introduced into the market in 1991. Therefore, at the time of sale, these products would have the whole market to themselves. We did believe that competitive products would be introduced in the fourth quarter of 1992, but those product-introductions would not be known at the time of the sale. Hence, our timing was perfect.

For the year ended March 31, 1991, Advanced Cooking Technologies had sales of $35 million and pretax profits of $8 million. Profits would have been significantly higher if the company had been able to control quality of the product (20% return rate from customers) and manufacturing costs. The company had acquired a number of new customers and was projecting sales of $90 million and profits of $20 million for the next fiscal year. At that time I told the owners that timing was perfect for a sale. Everything was going right for them, there were no clouds on the horizon, and the sale price would be between $200 and $250 million.

I proceeded to negotiate an engagement to represent Advanced in a sale. The board of directors of Advanced approved my engagement, but Bill Talburt was having second thoughts. He was having too much fun running the business. He totally disregarded approaching shadows in the form of competitive products that would be introduced in the next year.

Up to this point, Bill and his partners had been lucky despite the fact that the managerial skills of the owners of Advanced were not adequate to manage a business of $50 million to $200 million in sales. They were amateurs in terms of their manufacturing capabilities, since they were producing products with a high (20%) rate of defect at above-average cost. They had been lucky in developing the technologies they were selling, but had not been able to develop additional technologies or products to follow those they were currently selling. Bill Talburt prevailed on his partners to delay the sale for a few years so that they could enjoy the experience of running a fast-growing business. I knew they were making an incredible miscalculation, which would cost them tens of millions of dollars, but they would not listen to me.

In 1992 a number of competitive products were introduced to consumers. None of these products contained technology similar to that used by Advanced, but these products were all imported, and they were sold as being able to achieve the same cooking results at much lower retail prices. To meet the competitive challenge, Advanced had to reduce its selling prices and cut its profit-margins. Advanced continued to be plagued by problems with quality and ineffectiveness in production. Returns from customers continued to be at or above 20% of sales.

With competitive products in the market, customers like Wal-Mart, K-Mart, and Target threatened to drop products from Advanced and move to a competitive line unless problems with quality were eliminated. Advanced was unable to eliminate its problems with quality, and product costs continued to run out of control. Products from Advanced were taken off the shelf by most of its mass-market customers. For the year ended March 31, 1993, Advanced Cooking Technologies had sales of $37 million and pretax profit of $600,000, but with the loss of Wal-Mart, K-Mart, Target, and accounts with other large customers the company was projecting a large operating loss for the year ended March 31, 1994.

In April 1994, Bill Talburt called me and said, "Steve, we are ready to proceed with the sale of the company now. What do you think we can get for it?" After a thorough investigation I concluded that Advanced Cooking Technologies, a business that had been worth $200 to $250 million three years before, was now worth no more than $5 to $10 million. That is what I believed their technology could be worth to another player in the industry. They said they would not be interested in selling for that value, and continued to run the business until the spring of 1995, when they filed for a Chapter Seven bankruptcy liquidation proceeding.

You may say that this is a tragic story. Bill Talburt and his partners lost $200 to $250 million, because they didn't sell their business when you advised them to. Why are you ending your book with this story? What is the message you want to leave with us? I wrote this book in order to help you, the owner of a private business, maximize value at the time you decide to put your business up for sale. I discussed at length various ways to maximize value of the business, how to prepare the company for sale, who the buyers are, how to understand the way they think and how to find them, how the selling process works, how to sell without an asking price, and many other topics designed to give you the tools and the knowledge needed to get top dollar for your business when you decide to sell it. And I stressed that *a business should be sold when its value is peaking. The business value reaches its peak when its future looks the brightest.*

Bill Talburt and his partners were there. They were at the pinnacle of value for that business. It was worth $200 to $250 million. The owners knew that was the right time to sell. The owners knew that $200 to $250 million was an enormous price to obtain for this business. Conditions were right and timing was perfect. But they let opportunity pass them by, missing the score of a lifetime and ending up with nothing.

The message I am sending with this story is: *Don't wait to sell until it is too late, just because you are enjoying the ride, which is managing your business.* Remember what happened to Bill Talburt and his partners! Ownership of a business is full of risks. No one knows what will happen in the future. Any number of factors, such as competition, changes in technology, governmental regulations, problems with labor or environmental problems can negatively impact and decrease the value of your business. Many of these factors are beyond your control. Therefore, if you are contemplating being a seller — and I assume you are, or you would not be reading this book — never forget the example of Advanced Cooking Technology. *Never let this happen to you.* ⌒

When it comes to selling your business, you never want to say "I should have" or "I could have." When the time comes, and you know it is the right time: do it, sell it, and get on with the rest of your life.

TABLE SUMMARIZING THE FACTORS THAT MAXIMIZE VALUE OF A BUSINESS	
Factor	**Impact**
Selection of M&A advisor during selling process	An experienced advisor will have access to the buyers who will pay the most. The advisor will use proven selling techniques to obtain the maximum possible selling price.
Maximizing reported profits on financial statements	The tax savings from minimizing profits will be more than offset at the time of sale, because buyers pay multiples of reported earnings.
Recasting historical financial statements	Recasting increases profits by removing expenses that would not exist after the sale and increases book value by stating the true value of the assets of the business.
Auditing financial statements	Audits increase the credibility of the financial statements.
Having a strong managerial team	Buyers like companies with strong teams in management. A strong managerial team makes the business attractive to premium buyers who are not in the same business as the selling company.
Having a business plan	A credible plan can be used to sell the future, enabling the seller to get paid for projected profits that exceed historical profits. Buyers pay big premiums for growing companies.
Investing in equipment, systems, and facilities	Buyers like companies that are up-to-date. Conversely, they discount the value of companies where needed capital investments have been deferred. A company in state-of-the-art condition will attract more buyers to bid, resulting in a higher selling price.
Planning for capital expenditures	A consistent program for capital expenditures will result in a higher price for the seller. Without it, buyers will take a conservative approach and assume they will need to invest more than the seller would invest, to keep the business growing.
Having a diverse customer base	Buyers avoid or discount the value of companies with a few large customers dominating their business.
Timing the sale	The maximum value is obtained when the business's future looks the brightest. This may not coincide with the time the owner wants to sell.
Confidentiality	Any breach of confidentiality can damage the business.
Attempted sale to employees or competitors	These buyers seldom pay the highest prices. Dealing with them could reduce interest from other premium buyers.
Selling without an asking price	An asking price sets a limit on the value of the business. Let the competitive process and the market determine value.
Competitive auctioning process	Auctioning gives the advantage in negotiations to the seller by forcing buyers to make their best offers.

TABLE SUMMARIZING THE FACTORS THAT
MAXIMIZE VALUE OF A BUSINESS cont.

Factor	Impact
Liabilities	Paying down debt will maximize the cash received from the buyer. Prior to the sale, sell excess liquid assets and begin using profits to reduce liabilities.
Structure of the deal	The certainty of payment associated with the non-cash elements of a structured deal can have a huge impact on the ultimate value of the transaction.
Memorandum of Information	This document is essential to generate interest from buyers. It must be well crafted.
Liquid assets	A high percentage of liquid assets makes the deal more desirable and easier to sell because of the availability of financing.
Premium buyers	Buyers falling into this category will generally pay the highest price.

Glossary of Terms Used in Mergers & Acquisitions

All-cash transaction. Sale where 100% of the purchasing price is in the form of cash.

Annual cash flow. The net cash annually generated by a business. In many businesses, it is used as an indication for valuation, and multiples are applied to it to determine value of the business.

Balance sheet. A financial statement showing assets, liabilities, and ownership of net worth of a business.

Book value. Stated net worth of the company that may be less than the actual market value.

Capital expenditures. Money invested in capital improvements in the company.

Confidentiality agreement. An agreement that a potential buyer must enter into before being provided with confidential information on the selling company. The agreement commits the potential buyer to keep confidential all information provided during the sale process.

Customer concentration. When a business depends on a few large customers, that is "customer concentration." Buyers view businesses with customer concentration as being extremely risky and either avoid these companies entirely or make an offer with a substantial discount in the value.

Due diligence. An exhaustive investigation into all aspects of the company being sold. A thorough investigation with due diligence is performed by the buyer's representatives after they have signed a letter of intent and before they execute the purchase-and-sale agreement. The process of due diligence is also conducted by the seller's mergers-and-acquisitions advisor in preparation for marketing the business.

Earnouts. Given to the seller as part of the consideration (payout) for sale of the company. Earnouts are rights acquired by the seller to share in the future earnings of the company after the sale is completed.

EBIT. Earnings Before Interest and Taxes. In many sales, buyers develop their purchasing price by using multiples of EBIT.

EBITDA. Earnings Before Interest, Taxes, Depreciation, and Amortization. The EBITDA essentially represents the pre-tax cash flow generated by the business.

Exclusive Negotiations. When the business owner decides to negotiate with one buyer at a time for a limited time until an agreement is reached, that is exclusive negotiations.

Financial buyers. Buyers who acquire businesses as an investment in order to generate attractive returns on their investment by growing them and reselling them. Financial buyers' time horizons are short-term. Their goal is to sell in five to seven years.

Goodwill. The amount of the purchasing price that exceeds the value of the net assets purchased is called "goodwill."

Historical financial statements. Statements prepared in each of the two to three years before putting a business on the market are "historical at the time of the sale process."

Income statement. A financial statement showing the profitability of a business.

Letter of intent. A written agreement between the buyer and the seller that contains the principal business terms relating to the sale. Letters of intent typically bind the parties in two areas, confidentiality and exclusivity, and serve as a basis for preparing the purchase-and-sale agreement.

Leveraged recapitalization. A transaction in which the selling company is recapitalized with equity from a financial buyer, senior debt, and "mezzanine" debt. The seller is substantially cashed out using these sources of new funds, but, unlike an outright sale, the seller continues to maintain a substantial portion of the ownership in the business after the recapitalization is completed.

Limited auctioning process. Sales strategy using a competitive auctioning process with a limited number of interested parties.

Market value. The value of the business determined by the marketplace, using a competitive selling process.

Memorandum of Information. A detailed description of the selling company that is the first impression of the business for potential buyers. It is the single most important marketing tool used in the sales process.

Mezzanine lenders. Lenders who base their loans on the cash flow of the company but are junior in relation to security in assets of the company to the company's traditional lending bank. Mezzanine lenders usually bridge the gap between funds available through asset-based lending from banks and funds required to close the deal. Because of the high risk that they assume, mezzanine lenders charge rates of return that are 2.5 to 3 times those charged by other lenders.

Minimum net worth. The threshold amount of net worth that must remain in the business at the time of closing.

Non-compete agreement. A commitment given by the seller to the buyer stating that the seller will not compete in any way with the business being sold for an agreed upon term (3-5 years) after the sale.

Platform acquisition. The first acquisition made by a financial buyer desiring to consolidate an industry. The platform acquisition typically contains the managerial team who will represent the buyer in future additional acquisitions. Platform acquisitions typically sell for substantial premiums.

Premium buyers. Large organizations (public or private) with substantial financial resources who look for acquisitions in their industry or that fit into their strategic plan for growth.

Purchase-and-sale agreement. The definite agreement that controls the sale of the company. The agreement typically contains 50 or more pages and is the result of weeks of negotiations by the buyer's and seller's attorneys.

Put and Call. A mutual exchange of rights between buyer and seller to sell/acquire shares of stock within a specified period of time.

Recast financial statements. Financial statements in which the earnings have been increased by adjustments to add-back costs that would be eliminated after the company is purchased, such as excessive salaries to the owner, "perks," and aggressive tax accounting.

Recast net worth. An increase in net worth of the business being sold, to reflect the additional value created when the real market value of assets is greater than the book value.

Representations and warranties. Statements made by the seller about the condition of the business, its assets, liabilities, contracts, financial statements, and other areas that the buyer relied upon in making the decision to purchase. Representations and warranties typically survive the closing of the sale for one or two years and create potential liabilities for the seller.

Roll-up. A plan employed by financial buyers to consolidate an industry by completing a number of acquisitions, "rolled up together."

Royalties. Rights to receive specific payments over a period of years due to original interest in an intellectual property or other intangible.

Sale of assets. Transactions where the seller sells the assets of the business and the buyer assumes certain agreed-upon liabilities. All other liabilities of that business, whether actual or contingent, remain with the seller.

Sale of stock. A transactions in which the seller gives all of his or her shares in the company being sold in return for cash or other considerations.

Selling without an asking price. Technique used by sellers to obtain the highest possible price for their business. Rather than stating an asking price, the technique allows the market and competition among buyers to set the price.

Stock swap. A transaction in which the seller exchanges all of the stock in his or her private company for stock in a publicly traded company. The stock swap offers the seller the opportunity to defer tax on the gain until the publicly traded stock is sold.

Strategic buyers. Buyers who acquire only businesses related to their industry or that fit into their strategic operating plan. Strategic buyers make acquisitions designed to fit into a long-term plan.

Structured transaction. Sale where a significant percentage of the purchasing price is in the form of future payments, such as earnouts, notes, and non-compete payouts.

Subordinated notes. Notes that are part of the selling price given to the seller by the purchaser, without a guarantee by the purchaser as to repayment. Subordinated notes are subordinated to the rights of other lenders and depend upon the continued success of the business for repayment.

Success fee. The fee paid to the seller's mergers-and-acquisitions advisor upon the closing of the sale of the business. Success fees in mergers and acquisitions are contingent upon a closing and can be computed under a variety of formulas subject to agreement between the seller and his advisor.

Traditional auctioning process. Sales strategy using a competitive auctioning process in which the seller contacts a large number of potential purchasers. This strategy promotes maximum competition among buyers. ～

Appendix A: Checklist for Due Diligence

I. THE COMPANY

1. Description of the Business
- Main operations of the business
- Major product lines
- Method of operation
- Breakdown of product lines
- Other products and operations
- List of subsidiaries: location and percentage of ownership
- Seasonality and cyclicality of the business

2. Company History
- When founded and by whom
- Major milestones
- Acquisitions
  - Cost of acquisitions
  - Position of acquired company in the industry
  - Impact on sales of parent company after acquisition
- Recent financings, capital infusions, or other changes in capital structure
- Ownership
- Legal form of the business

3. Products
- Number
- Stability of product lines
- Major factors underlying volume of sales
- Seasonality
- Vulnerability to price-competition
- Vulnerability to obsolescence
- Present and potential production
- Capacity for producing main products compared with actual output in recent years
- Any governmental testing and regulatory problems with products

- Areas of market dominance. Why?
- Products with high or low margins
- Standard/custom products
- Length/number (units) of production runs
- Backlog
- Product warranty

4. Research and Development

- Importance to the Company and the industry of R&D
- R&D activities engaged in by the Company
- Number of employees in R&D
- Amount of expenditures for R&D over the last three to five years and amount forecast in next two to three years, broken down by type of research
- Amount funded in-house or by customers or third parties

5. Intellectual Property

- Dependence of the business on patents, brands, trademarks, copyrights
- Infringement suits

6. Customers

- List of major industries served by the Company and the percentage of last year's sales to each
- List of principal customers showing dollar sales and percentage of total sales for the last two years and an estimate of the number of other customers
- Any loss of customers to competitors in recent period
- Geographic distribution of sales
- Foreign sales

7. Sales/Distribution

- Type of system (own salesmen, distributors, number of branches, own warehouses)
- Amount of sales generated by outside sales reps
- System of compensation for sales force
- Training for sales force

- Turnover of sales force
- Marketing areas and location of warehouses and distributors

8. Advertising/Marketing
- Five-year breakout of advertising costs
- Plans for future advertising
- Representative/sample promotional material
- Other promotional methods (e.g., direct mail, telemarketing)

9. Pricing
- Price lists
- Price changes/approval process
- Discounting
- RFP (Request for proposal) response

10. Technology
- Type of manufacturing processes
- Proprietary expertise
- Degree of computerization/automation in product process (labor incentive)
- Capability in design and engineering
- Methods used in cost control
- Efficiency of production compared to their industry

11. Quality Control
- Number of personnel in QC
- Testing capability
- Equipment
- Certifications

12. Shipping
- Method of shipping used and any problems with shipping
- Shipping costs as compared with competitors' costs

13. Raw Materials and Purchased Parts of Units

- Relationship of important raw materials to any particular commodity or foreign source
- Source of raw materials; principal suppliers
- Contracts and pricing policy of suppliers
- Alternative sources of supply

14. Corporate Planning Process and Future Plans

- Corporate planning process
- Copy of business plan
- Planned capital expenditures or shutdowns
- New products and major improvements of present products
- New markets, plans and objectives for development
- Expansion of the product line
- Expansion of the customer base
- Investment needed for growth

15. Corporate Structure and Management

- Corporate and managerial organization chart
- Background of officers including age, years with the company, present position and past experience
- Contracts with personnel in management
- Quality and depth of management

16. Labor

- Labor required for production
- Type of labor pool tapped (skilled, unskilled)
- Union affiliations and expiration of contract
- Past labor relations (any strikes? If so, causes, duration, and outcome)
- Present labor relations
- Turnover of labor/management
- Number of employees; breakdown by function
- Average wages by department/job function
- Description of employee benefits, cost in percentage of wages

17. Property, Plant and Equipment
- Listing with brief description of principal PP&E
    - Size of plot (acres)
    - Size of buildings (square feet)
    - Age and type of construction
- Condition and age of major units of machinery for production
- Appraisals
- Copy of environmental review
- Tooling/dies — cost, value, ownership
- Cost of adding production capacity
- Replacement costs of machinery
- Outlook for future automation that may make current equipment obsolete

18. Rentals and Leases
- Aggregate obligations
- Description of production facilities, warehouses, and so forth that are under contract (leased)

II. INDUSTRY

1. General Description
- Size: sales volume and historical trends in the industry
- Product lines
- Customers
- History
- Major companies in the industry: size and location

2. Relationship of the Company to the Rest of the Industry
- Similarities
- Dissimilarities
- Percentage of market held by this Company in recent years
- Quality, performance, and breadth of Company as compared to competition
- Pricing policy of the Company compared with that of industry and major competitors

- Competitors' methods of distribution, recent changes in product-line, and capital expenditures

3. Outlook in this Industry
- Forecast for the market and expansion of this industry
- Competitor's future plans
- Membership in industry associations

4. Legislation
- Environmental Acts; problems with pollution (air and water) and related expenditures necessary to comply with rulings
- Expectation of any problems
- Any pending or proposed legislation with a material effect on the company and related expenditures necessary to comply with rulings

5. Competition
- Brief description of major competitors by product line
- Strengths and weaknesses of competitors
- Competitive advantage of client

III. OTHER

1. Litigation
- Any litigation pending or threatened; magnitude and possible outcome
- Contingent liabilities
- Any involvement by the Company or its officers in criminal proceedings, violations of regulations, commissions, or significant litigation in civil court

2. Insurance Coverage
- Major plant(s) and equipment
- Product liability
- Key personnel

3. General Community Relations
- Role of the Company in its community
- Emphasis on public relations

IV. FINANCIAL

1. Consolidated Balance Sheet

Historical
- Most recent five years of consolidated balance sheets and accompanying notes
- Balance sheet for most recent fiscal period
- Comments on balance sheets
- Consolidation method explained, including breakdown of subsidiaries
- Listing and explanation of any adjustments to historical balance sheets

Receivables
- Reserve for doubtful accounts, experience with write-offs
- Losses in each of last five years
- Trends in aging and collection period
- Normal terms
- Dating programs
- Procedures in credit management
- Accounts receivable aging summary — year end and interim

Inventories
- Method of valuation
- LIFO reserve, if any
- Problems with obsolescence
- Policy on write-downs and write-ups
- Trends in turnover
- Book to physical adjustments
- Past experience with inventory control
- Control systems for inventory
- Summary of inventory: year end and interim

Needs for Working Capital
- Seasonality
- Peak of short-term borrowings in past two years

Property, Plant and Equipment
- Depreciation method: book and tax
- Useful life used in depreciation schedule for building and equipment
- Tax/book value of PP & E

Investments and Other Assets
- Book value and market value
- Description of each

Goodwill
- How and when incurred
- Method of write-off

Current and Long-Term Debt
- Description of debt outstanding
  - Amount
  - Interest rate
  - Method of repayment
  - Date incurred
  - Maturity
  - Security
  - Present holders of debt
- Description of credit agreements with banks

Income Taxes
- Explanation of any years in dispute
- Possible additional assessments

Contingent Liabilities
- Explanation and breakout amounts of each, if any

Pensions
- Contributory portion and non-contributory portion
- Plans for hourly employees and for salaried employees
- Unfunded pension liability
- Method being used to fund
- How fund is managed

2. Consolidated Statement of Income

Historical
- Most recent five years of consolidated statements of income
- Statements of income for any major companies acquired for the years prior to their acquisition
- If not shown separately in statements, listing for each year
  - Unit sales (if practical and applicable)
  - Revenues from major product lines
  - Depreciation
  - Depletion
  - Amortization
  - Gross rentals
  - Interest paid on funded debt
  - Interest paid on current debt
  - Average number of employees
- Listing and explanation of any adjustments to historical income statements (e.g, owner's discretionary or non-recurring items)

Comments on Record of Earnings
- Explanation of trends in sales, operating profits, and earnings
- Explanation of poor years or losses, and remedial actions taken
- Relation of growth in sales to growth of industry
- Comments on:
  - Trends in margins
  - Any unusual operating profits or other income
  - Non-recurring profits or losses
  - Any extraordinary items and accounting treatments of them
- Policy on dividends, any large payouts

Rentals
- Brief description of policy concerning obligations for long-term leases (three years or longer) for:
  - Manufacturing properties
  - Warehouses
  - Sales offices
  - Manufacturing machinery
  - Office equipment
- Rental schedule of all leases having an original term of at least three years, including:
  - Date of lease
  - Term
  - Gross rent
  - Type of property
  - Option for renewal
  - Summary of minimum future payments on the leases and present value, if applicable

3. **Statement of Sources and Applications of Funds**

Historical
- Most recent five-year statements for flow of funds

4. **Projections**

Forecasts by Management
- Five-year projections of statements of income, statements of funds flow, and balance sheets
- Assumptions used
- Optimistic and pessimistic estimates and factors underlying these
- Comments by management on these projections ⌒

Appendix B. Example Memorandum of Information

BUCKEYE STATE PRINTING
C O N F I D E N T I A L
MEMORANDUM of INFORMATION

This Memorandum has been prepared by Buckeye State Printing ("BSP" or "The Company"), a subsidiary of Royal Corporation, a Delaware corporation, and Goldfarb Financial, Inc. ("Goldfarb"). This Memorandum is being delivered to a limited number of parties who may be interested in acquiring the Company, and its sole purpose is to assist the recipient in deciding whether to proceed with an in-depth study of the Company.

While the Company and Goldfarb have endeavored to include herein information they believe to be reliable and relevant, neither the Company nor Goldfarb makes any representation or warranty concerning the accuracy or completeness of such information, including, but not limited to, the financial forecasts included herein, or any other written or oral communication transmitted or made available to a prospective purchaser of the Company.

By accepting this Memorandum, the recipient agrees to keep confidential all information contained herein or made available in connection with any further investigation of the Company and to abide by such procedures relating to a possible purchase of the Company, as such procedures may be amended from time to time by the Company or Goldfarb, as the Company's exclusive representative. Further, unless prior written consent has been obtained from the Company or Goldfarb, or unless disclosure of the specific information is required by law and the recipient has so advised a responsible officer of the Company or from Goldfarb, the recipient agrees not to disclose to any person any Company information or the fact that any Company information has been made available, that discussions or negotiations are taking place concerning a possible transaction involving the Company, or any of the terms, conditions or other facts with respect to any such possible transaction, including the status thereof. The recipient also agrees that it will not contact, either directly or indirectly, any customer, supplier, competitor, employee, or any third party affiliated with or employed by the

Company to discuss the business of the Company, without first obtaining the written consent of the Company or Goldfarb.

This Memorandum shall not be photocopied, reproduced, or distributed to others at any time without the prior consent of the Company or Goldfarb. It has been delivered to prospective purchasers for informational purposes relating to a possible transaction and upon the express understanding that the recipient will use it only for the purpose set forth above. Upon request, the recipient will promptly return all material received from the Company or Goldfarb (including this Memorandum) without retaining any copies thereof. In furnishing the Memorandum, neither the Company nor Goldfarb undertakes any obligation to provide the recipient with access to any additional information.

No dealer, broker, salesman, or other person has been authorized to make any representations or give any information with respect to the Company, other than the representations and information set forth in the Memorandum and the other documents and information to be furnished upon request, as described herein. The information and opinions expressed herein are subject to change without notice. Neither the delivery of this Memorandum nor any participation in the acquisition shall, under any circumstances, create any implication that there has been no change in the operations or the financial affairs of the Company since the date hereof.

Qualified prospective investors or their representatives who have an interest in participating in the process of acquisition are asked to contact the following individuals:

Steven G. Goldfarb
Managing Director

TABLE OF CONTENTS

EXECUTIVE SUMMARY 154

Financial Highlights 155

Introduction 156

Reason For Sale 158

Investment Highlights 158

THE COMPANY 162

History 162

Products 163

Sales/Marketing 165

Customers 166

Suppliers 167

Organization 168

Equipment 171

Facilities 176

THE INDUSTRY 177

General 177

Industry Structure 178

Competition 179

FINANCIAL OVERVIEW 179

Management Discussion and Analysis 180

Pro Forma Assumptions 180

EXECUTIVE SUMMARY

The Company   Buckeye State Printing,
A subsidiary of the Royal Corporation.
Cleveland, Ohio

Business   Heatset and non-heatset printing of advertising inserts, newspapers and publications. 1998 revenues were divided as follows: advertising inserts, 65%, newspapers, 15%, publications, 15%, other, 5%.

Customers   A broad base of 500+ local newspapers, local publishers and
regional chains of retail stores.

Organization   A non-union workforce of 350. The Company is well managed
by a team that averages 11 years of experience with the
Company, and 18 years of experience within the printing
industry.

Equipment   Six Goss printing lines consisting of three heatset and three
non-heatset web presses. A seventh press line (a Goss C-700
heatset) will be added in August of 1999. Support equipment
consists of a full range of typesetting and key lining, prepress,
finishing and binding equipment. The Company had $20.0
million invested in machinery and equipment as of December
31, 1998, and has budgeted an additional $6.0 million for
capital investments in 1999.

Facilities   The Company owns a 150,000 square foot facility located on
11+ acres of land with ample room for expansion. The
Company had $3.7 million invested in facilities as of
December 31, 1998, and has budgeted an additional
$680,000 for capital investment in this regard in 1999.

Financial Highlights

		Historical			**Estimated**	**Projected**	
		1996	1997	1998	1999	2000	2001
Net Sales	$	36,673	41,598	43,650	49,913	54,413	59,513
Gross Margin							
	$	4,732	6,559	8,280	10,601	11,579	12,614
	%	12.9	15.8	19.0	21.2	21.3	21.2
Operating Income							
	$	2,241	3,448	4,781	7,081	7,950	8,743
	%	6.1	8.3	11.0	14.2	14.6	14.7

Buckeye State Printing
Historical Restated and Projected Income Statements
for Years Ended December 31
($000s)

Buckeye State Printing
Summary of Restated Balance Sheet
for Year Ended December 31, 1998
($000s)

Current Assets	$7,252	Current Liabilities	$4,544
Fixed Assets, Net	14,061	Long Term Liabilities	0
Other Assets	16	Total Liabilities	4,544
		Inter Co. Control Account	16,789
Total Assets	$21,333	Total Liabilities &	
		Inter Co. Control Account	$21,333

Introduction

Buckeye State Printing ("BSP" or "The Company") is a $50 million printer of advertising inserts, newspapers and publications. The Company is a subsidiary of Royal Corporation, a family-owned media company based in New York, which owns newspapers, television stations, and other media properties in several other states. The Company is located in Cleveland, Ohio.

BSP prints a wide variety of four-color and black-and-white jobs using either heatset or non-heatset capability. Advertising inserts account for 65% of revenues and are distributed by customers as supplements to Sunday or mid-week papers or as direct-mail pieces. The inserts typically advertise sales specials for regional retail merchandisers and grocery chains. The Company also prints 60 local tabloid-style newspapers, which account for 15% of sales. Publications such as low- to medium-volume monthly magazines and catalogs account for 15% of sales. Newspapers and publications are printed for local and regional publishers.

The Company has six Goss printing press lines. Three of the lines are heatset while three are non-heatset. Each press line is capable of on-line gluing and trimming. Other finishing capabilities include stitching, inserting, ink jet labeling, cheshire labeling, and binding. Most product (95%) is delivered using trucks owned by the Company to ensure timely and complete deliveries.

The market niche for BSP is providing outstanding customer service at extremely competitive prices for customers who do not require photographic quality in their printing. The Company can competitively run low-to-medium volume jobs ranging from 20,000 impressions to 8 million impressions. The Company has built a reputation as the premier printer of its type in the Cleveland area. The Company is renowned for completing and delivering work of consistent quality on time at the best price on the market.

The Company is well managed by a team that averages 11 years with The Company, and 18 years within the printing industry. Mr. William Clark, President, has been with The Company for 40 years, the last 20 as President. Current management has overseen the rise from a small local printer to a firm earning an 11% operating margin on sales of $44 million during 1998.

Reason for Sale

Royal Corporation is a New York-based media company that owns newspapers, television stations, and other media properties in several states. The management of Royal Corporation has determined that BSP does not fit with its strategic direction and wishes to divest in order to devote the full attention of management and company capital to the core media business.

Since its acquisition by Royal Corporation in 1993, BSP has operated as a standalone business and has management in place that wishes to remain with the Company after its sale.

Investment Highlights

There are numerous attractive qualities in BSP that a potential investor should consider when reviewing it as a candidate for acquisition.

Consistent Growth in Sales and Profitability. Sales have grown at an 11.6% compound growth rate to $44 million over the last four years. Pretax margins increased consistently during this time from 4.5% in 1994 to 11.0% in 1998. Growth in revenues is forecast to continue at 11% annually over the next three years to $60 million, principally on the basis of demand for a new Goss C-700 heatset press which is being installed in August. Operating margins are forecast to improve over the next three years to over 15%.

Growing Base of Customers Enhances Credibility of the Sales Forecast. The Company has added over 30 new customers during January and February, 1999, which generated $500,000 in additional sales volume. Most of these customers are promising repeat business monthly. In addition, the Company has generated interest in additional business pending the installation of the new C-700 press.

Competitive Advantage in Costs and Customer Service Through In-house Delivery. The Company delivers over 95% of its printed product with a fleet of radio-dispatched semi-trailers, trucks, and vans. Overnight service is offered to the surrounding five-state area. By controlling shipping, the Company ensures that all orders are delivered completely and on time. The Company is also able to quote extremely competitive shipping rates on destination cities where the Company is already sending trucks with less than truckload quantities.

Large Capital Investment Presents Formidable Barriers to Entry. The Company has an investment of $24.4 million in property, plant, and equipment as of December 31, 1998, and has budgeted an additional $6.7 million capital investment in 1999. This historical investment, significant ongoing capital expenditures, and the tremendous intangible costs it would take to duplicate customer relationships and the experience of management discourage new competitors from entering the industry.

Cost Advantage in Purchasing Paper Due to Diversity of Product Line. Because of BSP's broad base of printing, the Company purchases a variety of paper stocks in various widths. The ability to use odd lots and end-of-roll cuts of paper makes the Company a valuable customer to paper mills. Accordingly, BSP gets discounts on paper which it believes are as good as are offered to any other printer.

Outstanding Reputation for Quality and Service at Competitive Prices. BSP has built a reputation as the premier printer of its type in the Cleveland area, and it is renowned for completing and delivering work of consistent quality on time at the best price on the market.

As a Low-Cost Producer, BSP Earns Attractive Profits While Quoting Extremely Aggressive Prices. The Company believes it has a lower cost-structure than any of its competitors, due to its paper-purchasing advantage, efficient manufacturing operations, diverse base of non-seasonal business that continually keeps the equipment running, and captive trucking. As a result, BSP can bid extremely competitively and still earn exceptional profits.

In-house Finishing Capabilities. Perforating and/or on-line gluing and trimming are available on all press lines. The Company also offers automatic bundling, stitching, stacking, and tabbing, and ink-jet printing of bar codes and addresses for catalogs and other mailings. The Company also performs newspaper inserting for some customers.

Excellent Facilities with Room for Expansion. The 150,000 square foot facility for BSP was built in 1986 and is in excellent condition. A rail siding and seven shipping bays facilitate shipping and receiving. The Company's 11+ acre lot has ample room for expansion.

Experienced Management Team in Place Reduces Acquisition Risk for an Acquirer. The top managerial team averages 11 years of experience with BSP, and 18 years within the printing industry. The president has worked for the Company for 40 years, the most recent 20 years as president. At age 54, he plans to work for the Company for the foreseeable future.

Highly Motivated, Non-Union Workforce. The workforce at BSP is nonunion, which provides a competitive advantage through avoiding cumbersome working rules. Turnover is low, and the Company's reputation has been instrumental in attracting some of the most talented printing professionals in the industry.

THE COMPANY

History

The Company, originally named Crown Publishing, was founded in 1946 by Mr. Carl Smith as a publisher of the Buckeye State News. In addition to printing its own weekly paper, Crown also printed some commercial work with sheet fed printing capability. William Clark, currently president, joined the Company in 1958 in the maintenance department. In 1962, at age 18, Mr. Clark was named foreman of printing operations. He worked in a variety of production positions and was named president in 1978.

The Company grew steadily in the 1970s and 1980s. In 1981, The Company was awarded the sales circular business for a large national retailer, its first job printing inserts. Annual Company billings were $500,000. In 1983, after adding an additional press and a 10,000 square foot expansion, the Company began to run around-the-clock shifts. Also in 1983, BSP sold the Buckeye State News and the commercial sheet-fed printing business, to focus on web printing. During 1985, William Clark purchased the business. The Company continued to prosper during the 1980s, growing from $3 million in revenue in 1985 to $27 million in 1991. All of the printing at this time was non-heatset.

In 1988, BSP moved to its present location. Since the move, The Company has increased square footage under occupancy several times, to accommodate continuous growth. The Company currently occupies 150,000 square feet.

In 1991, BSP added its first heatset press to expand into additional capability for printing inserts.

In 1992, Royal Corporation purchased BSP. Since the buyout, under William Clark's continuing management, sales increased to $44 million and operating profits to $4.8 million by 1998. With the pending purchase of a state-of-the-art Goss C-700 heatset press, the Company is well positioned to continue to grow on a profitable basis under new ownership.

Products

Buckeye State Printing is a printer of advertising inserts, local newspapers, and publications such as directories and catalogs. The Company specializes in printing low- to medium- volume runs for customers who demand outstanding customer service and extremely competitive pricing, yet do not require printing of high photographic quality. Types of products produced by BSP are described in more detail below:

Advertising Inserts. The Company prints promotional pieces for retailers, which are typically distributed as a supplement to the Sunday paper. Some inserts are mailed. Most inserts are four-colored. While inserts can be printed on non-heatset presses, the trend is moving toward heatset. Inserts are BSP's highest volume printing jobs, with weekly run-sizes ranging from several hundred thousand up to eight million. Weekly job-sizes range from $10,000 to $180,000 weekly, with an average job-size of $15,000. Inserts account for approximately 65% of the Company's revenues.

Newspapers. Approximately 60 tabloid-style weekly and monthly papers for 34 customers are printed by BSP. All of the papers are local and are based in Ohio. Newspapers are typically printed in small runs ranging from several thousand to 100,000 copies and averaging 20,000 copies. Job-sizes range from $400 to $20,000 weekly, with an average job-size of $6,000. The papers are mostly black and white with some four-colored pictures. Newspapers account for about 15% of revenues.

Publications. Monthly tabloid-style magazines are also printed by BSP. The publications differ from newspapers in that they generally have colored covers that are printed on a heavier paper stock than the rest of the publication. The average run-size is 40,000 to 50,000 copies. Job-sizes range from $3,000 to $25,000 with an average job-size under $10,000. Most of the publications are printed on non-heatset presses, but heatset presses are used for some issues with the larger runs (350,000 to 500,000 copies). Publications are usually printed for local publishers and account for approximately 15% of the revenues of the Company.

Other. The Company prints school directories and industrial catalogs. Similar in appearance to publications, directories and catalogs have a cover, usually colored, which is printed on heavier paper stock than the text. Directories and catalogs range in run-size from 10,000 to 500,000 copies and account for 5% of sales.

Quality is an extremely important aspect of the business and is marketed by the sales force to differentiate BSP from its competitors. The quality department reviews all critical artwork and film, prior to initialization of a job. This procedure ensures that production begins with an inspecting procedure of high integrity. In the prepress department, job-proofers are scheduled 24 hours a day, seven days a week. These proofers review all initial press-proofs, all changes in versions and proofs from all folders, at every shift-change. Long run or highly critical jobs also undergo plate-proofing scrutiny prior to startup of the presses.

The 24-hour staff of customer service employees at BSP routinely pulls proofs from all areas of production throughout their shifts to inspect for pagination, ink-settings, registration, and trim-size. The Company's newly installed ink-lab will soon be providing a host of quality testing procedures along with ink-mileage tests and draw-down capabilities. The Company's paper-warehouse manager works directly with technicians from each of its major suppliers. The mills' technicians routinely visit the plant and perform both visual testing and porosity testing for sheet formation and tear strength. The Company has also established committees for maintenance of equipment in each of the production departments, to review and improve on the condition and capabilities of each major machine in production.

In addition to quality, customer service is an important competitive factor by which BSP distinguishes itself. In-house finishing capabilities and captive delivery trucks enable BSP to offer superior customer service. Perforating and/or on-line gluing and trimming is available on all press lines. The Company also offers automatic bundling, stitching, newspaper inserting, stacking and tabbing, and printing of ink-jet bar codes and addresses for catalogs and other mailings.

Outstanding customer service is also provided by BSP through in-house delivery of products. The Company delivers over 95% of its printed product with a fleet of radio-dispatched semi-trailers, trucks, and vans. Overnight service is offered to the surrounding four-state area. By controlling shipping, the Company ensures that all orders are delivered completely and on time. The Company is also able to quote extremely competitive shipping rates on destination cities where it is already sending trucks with less-than-truckload quantities.

Sales/Marketing

A direct sales force of seven people is employed by BSP. They generate 94% of Company revenues. Most of the sales force is compensated through a salary-plus-commission structure, which ranges from .25% to 3% of sales volume. The Company recently opened a one-man sales office in Chicago to concentrate on national accounts. National accounts are customers that distribute their printing, typically inserts or large catalog mailings, in multiple states and therefore are more open to using an out-of-state printer. The Company anticipates that national accounts will be a large contributor to future growth, as many of these prospective customers will be attracted by the new Goss C-700 press heatset printing capability.

BSP attends one trade show annually, the Retail Advertisers Trade Fair in Chicago, at which large mass retailers attend to shop for media. Annual spending on trade show and other forms of advertising and promotion is approximately $40,000. These expenditures have been kept to a minimum due to the Company's strong market identity and outstanding reputation for quality, price, and service.

Customers

The Company's customers consist of a broad base of local newspapers, local publishers, and regional chains of retail stores. Most of the Company's 500-plus customers are longstanding and continue to do business with the Company because of its consistent quality, outstanding customer service, and competitive pricing. Listed below are the 20 largest customers.

Customer Sales by Type of Product ($000)

Customer[1]	Job	1996 $	%	1997 $	%	1998 $	%	Customer Since
Customer A	Insert	9,252	24.6	10,858	25.8	11,893	26.9	1988
Customer B	Newspaper	3,951	10.5	3,448	8.1	3,442	7.7	1982
Customer C	Insert	249	.6	2,781	6.6	2,772	6.2	1991
Customer D	Insert	1,922	5.1	1,671	3.9	1,798	4.0	1990
Customer E	Insert	1,107	2.9	953	2.2	1,151	2.6	1990
Customer F	Insert	1,627	4.3	540	1.2	1,091	2.4	1990
Customer G	Newspaper	769	2.0	713	1.6	761	1.7	1979
Customer H	Insert	856	2.2	476	1.1	731	1.6	1993
Customer I	Newspaper	813	2.1	642	1.5	710	1.6	1989
Customer J	Newspaper	724	1.9	746	1.7	669	1.5	1983
Customer K	Insert	625	1.6	649	1.5	661	1.4	1991
Customer L	Publication	390	1.0	629	1.4	600	1.3	1982
Customer M	Publication	202	.5	492	1.1	582	1.3	1985
Customer N	Insert	310	.8	375	.8	509	1.1	1993
Customer O	Publication	357	.9	351	.8	444	1.0	1989
Customer P	Insert	437	1.1	399	.9	433	.9	1990
Customer Q	Insert	383	1.0	381	.9	399	.9	1993
Customer R	Newspaper	100	.2	440	1.0	384	.8	1990
Customer S	Publication	0	0	369	.8	379	.8	1992

Sales are primarily concentrated in the Midwest, particularly in Ohio and Michigan. The table below summarizes revenues by state for the first quarter of 1998.

Geographic Distribution of Sales

Ohio	49.1%
Michigan	29.0%
Pennsylvania	5.1%
Illinois	3.2%
Iowa	2.9%
Indiana	2.8%
Kentucky	2.7%
Other	5.2%
	100.0%

Suppliers

The largest cost item used by BSP is purchased paper. Approximately 40,000 tons of paper was purchased in 1998 at a cost of $19.2 million. The largest usage is of 30-lb. newsprint paper for non-heat printing. Paper is purchased from multiple sources, and BSP receives competitive purchasing discounts due to the high volume and wide variety of paper stock it purchases. The Company's ability to use odd widths of paper makes it a valuable customer to mills who typically cater to customers with more uniform purchasing requirements that generate a lot of scrap.

The item with the second largest cost is ink. More than 1.2 million pounds of black, red, yellow and blue inks were used in 1998, at a cost of $1.9 million. The Company purchases ink from one supplier, although alternative sources are available. Soy inks are used for colors for all processes due to the superior quality and favorable environmental characteristics.

Organization

The Company is well managed by a team that averages 11 years with the Company. Listed below are biographies of key members of the managerial team.

President (Age 54)

The president is responsible for the overall operating performance and strategic direction. His background is in production. He joined the Company in 1958 in the maintenance department. After gaining experience in the press department, he was named foreman in 1962. Through several changes in ownership, he acted as general manager. In 1978 he was named to his current position of president.

Sales Director (Age 33)

The sales director is responsible for development of business and for maintaining existing business. In addition to managing a sales staff of eight, he also has direct responsibility for several large house accounts. In 1994, his efforts led to the awarding of business from the Company's largest customer, which today generates in excess of $11 million in annual sales. He joined the Company in 1986 as a salesman.

Director of Administration (Age 32)

The director of administration is responsible for all administrative matters of the Company including management information systems, legal compliance, environmental compliance, payroll, and benefits. He also assists with setting short-term and long-term business operating strategy. Prior to joining the Company in 1991, he worked in management for a large national retailer.

Controller (Age 30)

The controller is responsible for financial reporting and budgeting. She is also responsible for invoicing and collections, purchasing, and management of accounts payable. She joined the Company in 1992 after three years in public accounting.

Production Director (Age 34)

The production director has responsibility for profits in the Press and Prepress Departments. He also oversees scheduling of production, maintenance of presses, and budgeting for capital equipment. He joined BSP in 1988 and has five years of prior experience in related work.

Director of Quality (Age 51)

The Director of Quality is responsible for the quality and integrity of all jobs for BSP. She facilitates training in quality control, and integrity of proof and copy, and reviews and makes recommendations on all customer complaints. She joined the Company in 1987 and had 22 years of prior related experience.

The following table shows employment in areas of production and average wage rates by department.

Hourly Employment in Production by Department		
Department	Employees*	Weighted Average Wage
Prepress	42	$12.99
Press	165	$11.46
Finishing	48	$9.07
Shipping/Warehouse/Maintenance	32	$11.24
	287	

*Excludes 11 salaried supervisors in the prepress and press departments. Also excludes 43 part-time employees in finishing who earn an average hourly wage of $7.61.

In addition to the 287 production-related employees described above, BSP employs 46 nonproduction employees and 11 salaried employees in production for a total full time employment of 344. All full time employees are offered a comprehensive benefits package including medical and dental insurance, life and disability insurance, and profit-sharing. BSP also offers a 401k plan without matching. Benefits totaled 34.7% of wages in 1998.

Currently, BSP runs four 12-hour shifts in press and prepress and three 8-hour finishing shifts. Each shift works four days (or nights) in a row, with four days (or nights) off. The plant runs 24 hours daily, seven days weekly. The Company is currently running at 80% of capacity.[1]

Equipment

As of December 31, 1998, BSP had $20.0 million invested in machinery and equipment. Most of this investment consists of three heatset and three non-heatset Goss presses. The Company also has a complete line of typesetting and keylining, prepress, finishing, and binding equipment. In 1999, BSP has budgeted a $6.0 million investment in machinery and equipment, the bulk of which represents the addition of a Goss C-700 heatset press and press-related equipment. The following table lists major pieces of machinery and equipment in the press department. Please refer to the equipment list in Exhibit III for a complete list of pre-press, press, finishing, shipping, and miscellaneous equipment.

---

[1]Capacity is defined as 24 hours daily x 7 days weekly. The Company believes that exceeding 85% of capacity would be difficult due to required down time for press maintenance.

Non-Heatset	Heatset
Line I: 20　Goss Community Units, 22 3/4" Cut-off, Maximum Roll Width 35" (8 of these units are 4-high stacks) 3　Goss SSC Combination Quarter Folders 1　Ribbon Deck 15　Roll Stands 1　Enkel Roll Splicer **Line II:** 16　Goss Community Units, 22 3/4" Cut off, Maximum Roll Width 35" (4-4 high stacks) 3　Goss SSC Combination 1/4 folders 1　Double Ribbon Deck 5　Enkel Rollsplicers 2　Enkel Web Aligners **Line III:** 16　Goss C-150 Units, 21 1/2" Cut-off, Maximum Roll Width 35" (4-4 high stacks) 3　Goss C-150 Combination Quarter Folders (Double Parallel Fold w/ Crosshead Perf. Avail. on One) 2　Ribbon Decks 5　Enkel Roll Splicers w/ Infeeds	**Line I:** 8　Goss C-150 Units, 21 1/2" Cut-Off, Max. Roll Width 35" (2-4 high stacks) 2　Goss C-150 Folders 1　1/2 & Double Parallel Folder 1　Combination 1/2 & 1/4 Folder 2　TEC Dryers 2　TEC Chillstands 1　Double Ribbon Deck 1　Single Ribbon Deck 2　Martin Automatic Roll Splicers with Infeeds 2　Quad Tech RGS IV Register and Cut-off Control Units **Line II:** 8　Goss C-500 Units, 21" Cut-off Max. Roll Width 40" 3　Goss C-500 Folders, 1 w/Double Parallel & Crosshead Perf. 1 w/ 1/2 Fold Stitcher 1　Duplexing Package 2　19' Thermo Electron Dryers w/Chill Stands 2　Martin Automatic Roll Splicers 1　On-line Letterpress Imprinter (uses adhesive backed plates) 2　Goss Colortrol Systems 1　Tobias Plate Scanner, Combined w/ Control Units for Automatic Ink Settings 1　Former Bypass Unit 2　Quad Tech RGS IV Register and Cut-off Control Units **Line III:** 4　Goss Magnum Units, 21" Cut-off, Max. Roll Width 35" 1　Goss Magnum Folder w/Double Parallel & 1/4 Fold 1　Tech Dryer w/ chill stand 1　Enkel Splicer and Infeed 1　Colortrol system 1　Quad Tech Register & Cut-off Control

The following table lists major pieces of machinery and equipment in the finishing department.

Finishing Equipment

1	McCain S-2500, 5-Pocket w/Card Feeder, High-Speed Saddle Binding System, 3-4-5 Knife Capabilities
1	McCain 2000XL 9-Pocket Stitcher Trimmer with Cover Feeder, 3-4-5 Knife Capabilities, Rima Compensating Stacker
1	McCain 1800 2-Pocket Stitcher with Cover Feeder
1	Seybold 42" Cutter
1	Muller Martini: High-Speed 8-into-1 (1/4-or 1/2-Fold) Inserter with Hopper Loader w/ Counter Stacker
1	Muller Martini: 2-into-1 (1/4-or 1/2-Fold) Inserter
1	Muller Martini: 5-into-1 (1/4-or 1/2-Fold) Inserter
1	Muller Martini: 10-into-1 (1/4-or 1/2-Fold) Inserter w/ Hopper Loader and Counter Stacker
1	Kurk Rudy Prism Fully Automatic Ink-Jet System with Tabber & Ramp Stacker & Cross Strappers
1	Kurk Rudy Labeler 3, 4, & 5 Up Capabilities
1	Cheshire Labeler 596 Back & 539 Head
1	Signode Automatic Box-Sealer
1	GUK 2k-500 Automatic Knife Folder w/Crusher Unit
1	Kansa 1/4 Folder
1	Muller Martini 241 6-Pocket Stitcher w/ 3-4-5 knife capabilities and Rima Stacker

Capital expenditures for machinery and equipment over the last three years have averaged $1.5 million annually. Most expenditures have been to replace and upgrade equipment in the press room. The following table illustrates historical capital expenditures by year and highlights significant expenditures.

Historical Capital Expenditures
($000)

Item	Department	Amount
1996		
C-500 Folder	Press	$402
Water Osmosis System	Press	117
Other	Press	<u>426</u>
		$945
1997		
Blanket Wash System	Press	228
Goss Magnum Press	Press	1,628
Ink Jet System	Mailing	151
Signode Automatic Bander	Packaging	162
Building Purchase	Building	3,712
Other	Binding, Press, Camera	<u>602</u>
		$6,483
1998		
Inserter	Inserting	346
Shredder/Baler	Warehouse	140
Other	Binding, Press Composition, Warehouse	<u>344</u>
		$830

Budgeted Capital Expenditures
($000)

Item	Department	Amount
1999		
Goss C-700 Heatset Press (4 units, 2 folders including installation)	Press	3,860
Stitcher Trimmer	Finish	685
Mesomix Step and Repeat Machine	Prepress	235
Purup Image Maker	Prepress	232
Stackers	Press	139
Building Expansion	Building	680
Other	Various	<u>882</u>
		$6,713

BSP has not had regular capital budgets in the traditional sense of an anticipated annual plan against which variances were measured and explained. Rather the "capital budgets" have been lists of equipment that might be employed, depending on developments in the marketplace. The purpose of these "budgets" is to initiate dialogue and enable contingency planning. Historically, the Company has never spent all of the money in its "capital budget," and even some items of equipment represented by BSP to Royal Corporation as "definite needs" were approved but never purchased. Accordingly, the following capital forecasts are conservative and should be interpreted in the proper context.

Net capital expenditures totaling $6.3 million are forecast over the next two years to support growth of revenues to $60 million by 2001. The following table summarizes possible expenditures by year, and highlights the most significant expenditures:

Projected Capital Expenditures ($000)		
Item	Department	Amount
2000		
Goss Magnum Press (8 units, 4 folders)	Press	3,200
Sale of Goss C150 Press (Replaced by Goss C-700, Magnums)	Press	<1,700>
Lino Output-full page	Prepress	250
Step and Repeat	Prepress	160
Stitcher Auxiliary Equipment	Finish	450
Other	Press, Prepress	190
		$2,550
2001		
Replace SSC Press Line	Press	2,500
Building Expansion	Building	500
Other	Press, Prepress	750
		$3,750

Facilities

The Company owns a 150,000 square-foot facility located on 11.27 acres of land in an industrial park in Cleveland, Ohio. The building is a single story and was constructed in stages beginning in 1984. Today the building encompasses approximately 5,800 square feet of office space and 121,000 square feet of warehouse and shop space. The building is constructed of concrete tilt up and concrete block walls.

The Company moved into the facility in 1988. Since the move, BSP has increased the square footage under occupancy several times to accommodate its continuous growth. A rail siding and seven shipping bays facilitate receiving and shipping. The land and building were purchased by the Company in May, 1996, for $3.7 million. An environmental review was conducted at the time, which indicated that the facility is free of environmental problems.

The Company forecasts a 10,000 square foot expansion of the building during 1999 at a cost of $600,000, to accommodate the new Goss C-700 press. An expansion of the offices and a redesign the prepress and customer service areas in 2001 is forecast at a cost of $500,000.

THE INDUSTRY

General

According to the *U.S. Industrial Outlook 1999,* shipments of the U.S. printing and publishing industry should increase to $177 billion during 1999, an increase of nearly 2% over 1998 in constant dollars. An improved economy and gains in advertising expenditures, which affects two-thirds of industry shipments, are responsible for the increase. Other factors affecting demands for printing are disposable personal income, formations of businesses, and appropriations for schools, libraries, and institutions. The U.S. is the world's largest market for printed products, and a favorable set of demographic trends during the next several years should reinforce this position.

Listed below is a discussion on the trends in the markets for BSP's specific products:

Newspapers. Shipments of newspapers are projected to grow by 5.4% during 1999, to $37.8 billion from $35.9 billion in 1998, according to the U.S. Industrial Outlook 1999. U. S. weekly newspapers have fared better than dailies. While total numbers dropped from 7417 in 1997 to 7406 weeklies in 1998, circulation increased from over 54 million to more than 55 million during the same time period.

Commercial Printing. The *U.S. Industrial Outlook 1999* states that shipments of commercial printing grew by 2.9% from $51.1 billion in 1997 to $52.6 billion during 1998. Shipments are forecast to grow by 6.1% to $55.8 billion during 1999. Printed advertising, including newspaper inserts, totaled $21 billion in 1998, accounting for 40% of the U.S. market for commercial printing. More than 90% of printed advertising materials are manufactured by the lithographic (web) process.

Revenues from printing of magazines totaled $7.4 billion in 1998, an increase of almost 2% from 1997. Printing of magazines accounts for 14% of total printing shipments, with all but the largest publications printed by the lithographic process. Gravure printers, with presses geared to print runs exceeding

1 million copies per issue, have contracts to print virtually all U.S. comic books and about one-half of the 20 largest U.S. consumer publications.

Shipments of printed catalogs and directories surged 3% in 1998 to $6.3 billion. The gradual disappearance of large, mass-audience catalogs has not had a significantly adverse effect. Such publications have been replaced by multi-mailings of more sharply focused catalogs, targeted to receptive niche markets. Printing of catalogs and directories represents 12% of total shipments in the industry, with all but the largest publications printed by lithography.

Structure of the Industry

The printing industry is highly fragmented and moderately concentrated at the top. In 1993, there were approximately 40,000 printers in the United States per the *Printing 2000 Report.* The vast majority (about 32,000) are small firms with annual revenues below $2 million and fewer than 20 employees. At the top of the industry, the ten largest printers have about 14% of the printing business. The table below shows the overall structure of the industry.

Structure of the Printing Industry

Structure of the Printing Industry	# of Firms	Total Share of Commercial Printing Market
$50+ Million	150	40%
$10 - 50 Million	500	16%
$2 - 10 Million	7,500	24%
Under $2 Million	32,000	20%
	40,000	100%

Generally, the industry will become more concentrated at the top. The very largest printers will have distinct competitive advantages such as economies of scale, better access to capital, and better depth in management. At the same time, the smallest printers, who currently have about 20% of all commercial printing activity, will maintain distinct advantages by catering to the needs of local markets.

Competition

The following table lists competitors to BSP by type of production.

List of Competitors (By Type of Publication)		
Insert	**Publication**	**Newspaper**
Heat Set:	**Heat Set:**	
Company 1	Company 2	Company 3
Company 4	Company 5	
Company 6		
Company 7	**Non-Heat:**	
	Company 8	
Non-Heat:		
Company 9		
Company 10		

FINANCIAL OVERVIEW

Restated historic and projected statements of income for BSP are shown on Schedules 1 and 1A in dollars and percentages, respectively. Schedules 2 and 2A illustrate an analysis of variable and fixed costs in dollars and percentages, respectively. The Company's historic and projected balance sheets are presented on Schedule 3. Schedule 4 shows historic and projected balance sheets in percentages. The Company's historic and pro forma statements of cash flow are illustrated in Schedule 5. Finally, Schedule 6 analyzes the historic and projected accounts for property, plant, and equipment.

Discussion and Analysis by Management

Revenues. Revenues for BSP have grown from $36.7 million in 1996 to $43.7 million in 1998, representing 9.1% compound annual growth. While BSP has been very successful at retaining long-term customers, many of whom have increased their volumes of business over the years, recent growth has largely been driven by the addition of new customers. Twelve of BSP's 20 largest customers have been added in the last four years. These customers accounted for $10.7 million, or 24.5% of business during 1998. As discussed throughout this document, BSP is a formidable competitor due to its ability to deliver quality product with outstanding service at the most competitive price in the market.

Variable Expenses. Paper is the largest component of expenses, its cost totaling 44.1% of sales in 1998. Costs for paper have declined from 46.4% of sales in 1996, due to over-capacity in the paper industry and the resulting softness in prices of paper. Costs for ink have decreased from 4.6% of sales in 1996 to 4.1% of sales in 1998. Decreases in price and a 1998 conversion to soy ink are responsible for the decline.

Fixed Expenses. Depreciation decreased from 5.3% of sales in 1996 to 3.9% of sales in 1998. Rent decreased to zero due to the 1997 purchase of the manufacturing facility.

Pro Forma Assumptions

Revenues. Revenues are forecast to grow by 10.9% annually over the next three years, from $43.7 million in 1998 to $59.5 million in 2001. The Company plans to add a Goss C-700 heatset press during 1999, which will be the primary contributor to continued growth.

Variable Costs. Costs for paper are forecast to remain close to current levels. The Company forecasts a modest rise from the current projection of 42.3% of sales in 1999 to 42.4% of sales by 2001. Costs for ink are forecast to rise modestly from 4.1% of sales in 1998 to 4.3% of sales by 2001 because of the growing volume of heatset work. Heatset printing requires more colored inks than non-heatset printing.

Productive labor is currently running at a rate of 15.2% of sales. The Company forecasts that this expense will decline to 13.6% of sales by 2001 due to the use of more sophisticated prepress equipment and the increase in heatset printing. Labor is a smaller component of heatset printing because of the faster press speeds and higher selling price of the product.

Other operating costs totaled 2.1% of sales in 1998. The largest component of this expense, bad debts, is expected to decline to 1% of sales due to better collection procedures recently implemented, including a new hire in accounting who will be dedicated to collections. Consequently, other operating costs are forecast to decline to 1.7% over the next three years.

Fixed Costs. Other costs for employees are forecast to rise from 7.0% of sales in 1998 to 7.4% of sales in 2001. No significant increases are forecast in the other categories of fixed cost. ⌒